THE FISHLADY'S®
COOKBOOK

The World's Easiest Seafood Cookbook
by
Patricia Kendall

First published in the United States of America in 1998 by
Octavo Press an imprint of
Templegate Publishers
302 East Adams Street
Springfield, Illinois 62701
217-522-3353
www.templegate.com

ISBN 0-87243-236-X
Library of Congress Catalog Card Number 98-60111
Front cover: Bord Failte - Irish Tourist Board

This book is dedicated to all the fish-lovers of the world and to the children who gave me the name "The Fishlady."

Introduction

Hello! I'm the Fishlady. I'm so glad you decided to pick up this book. Inside these pages I'm going to teach you the basics of cooking seafood and you'll see how easy it will be for you to become the expert. Why me? Well, because I see fish everyday. I preside over a splendid fish counter at a large supermarket and have seen people who are intimidated by fish for too long! So that's why.

Over the years I have written a column on cooking fish, conducted classes at a community college and given countless demonstrations. I do not claim to be a gourmet cook like Craig Claiborne or the editors of *Larousse Gastronomique*, the ultimate book on food. But most of us work outside the home these days and after a long day we don't want to spend more long hours in the kitchen preparing complicated dishes! But we do want to provide balanced and nutritious and delicious meals.

So we will start right now—at the fish counter or frozen fish aisle in your favorite grocery store.

The question most often asked about fish is:

Q. How much fish should I buy for one person?

A. 6 to 8 ounces of fish fillet is adequate.

Now you're home in the kitchen and as you're unwrapping the fish you ask:

Q. What do I do with it?

A. You can cook this fish many different ways:

1. microwave
2. bake
3. broil
4. grill
5. sauté
6. steam
7. poach
8. fry
9. oven-fry

Yes, you can use all these methods for the same fish.

Another question everyone asks is:

Q. How can I tell when the fish is done?

A. Flakiness. If the fish fillet will flake easily with a fork, it's done.

Now put away all those seafood recipes that you would never even attempt to cook because they seem too difficult. Come with me right now into the wonderful world of easy seafood cooking. I'm going to show you how to take your favorite fish fillet and prepare it many ways—changing the flavor every time. This as I've said is the easiest seafood cookbook you'll ever find.

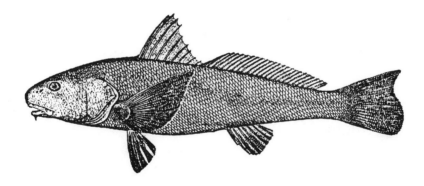

FISH RECIPES

TABLE OF CONTENTS

About Fish

Fish has been around since the earth was created. Fish is the healthiest food to eat. Many stores are now putting in seafood shops.

Then why do we shy away? Why do we say we don't like fish? It is because we always thought fish was too smelly or had to be deep fried to be good and that seemed very messy.

This book will change all that. People who have always said they don't like fish will find that they do like it — once they know how to cook it.

Many seafood shops are turning to Farm-Raised Seafood because so many rivers and streams are polluted. The fish are raised on a fish farm. They are fed in a controlled environment. Many stores get their seafood IQF, which means Individually Quick Frozen, from many different places such as Greenland, Chile, New Zealand and Antarctica. They are caught in very deep, icy waters that are unpolluted. The most popular variety is orange roughy, a deep-sea perch. Its flesh is white, the rough skin is bright orange.

Those little critters with gills and flippers known as "fish" come in all sizes, shapes and colors. If I had to list every fish in the sea I'd be here forever! So here's my list and description of the most common and recognizable:

Carp — A very bony, fishy flavor. Once filleted, it must be scored because it has very small bones still left. Scoring cuts the bones so small they cook away when frying. To score a carp fillet, use a fillet knife to make long length-wise close cuts through the flesh, almost through the skin. This fish is best fried in batter.

Ocean Catfish — A delicate white meat fish that is good baked or broiled.

Cod — one of the lowest in fat — a firm yet mild white meat that lends itself to any method of cooking and is great in chowders and stews.

Flounder — A delicate, mild flavor that's good for the dieter. Best poached or microwaved.

Grenadier — A new fish to the markets. It has a sweet mild buttery flavor and is good oven-baked.

Grouper — Has a sweet, mild flavor and is a good fish for baking.

Haddock — Another fish good for weight-watchers. It has a delicate mild flavor and is good poached, baked or microwaved.

Halibut — Mild, meaty flavor that is good grilled or blackened and especially good in stews and chowders.

Lake Superior Whitefish — Has a fishy flavor and is very bony. This fish is good broiled or in a fish boil with carrots, onions and potatoes.

Mahi-mahi — A fish so good they named it twice. It is beige in color and has a meaty chicken-like consistency that suits it for the grill.

Ocean Perch — A strong fish flavor and is best fried or oven-fried.

Orange Roughy — White meat, delicate, mild yet meaty. Becoming the most popular fish around because of its delicious flavor. This fish can be cooked just about any way.

Oreo-Dory — Similar in taste to orange roughy but just a little firmer and stronger and about half the price. Good grilled, fried or oven-fried.

Pomfret — It tastes like chicken and is great in a stir-fry.

Red Snapper — Similar in taste to grouper but a little stronger and firmer. It's good for the grill or blackened.

Salmon — A distinct flavor all its own. Strong but not fishy. The fish oil in salmon helps to rid the arteries of plaque build-up. Very good for diets and lends itself to any method of cooking but more frequently is baked, poached or grilled.

Sole — Very delicate, thin, white meat fish that is mild and best poached, baked, steamed, or microwaved.

Shark — Firm, meaty with a pork-like consistency. I refer to it as a greaseless pork chop. This fish will not flake when cooked, rather smooth and tender to the cut and wonderful for the grill.

Swordfish — Firm, meaty and flaky when cooked and great on the grill or broiled.

Tilapia — A fish quite new to the markets isn't really new at all because some legends identify it as the fish Christ served to the multitudes. Now in this country, it's farm-raised, similar in taste and texture to catfish but a little more delicate. Very good baked, poached or broiled.

Rainbow Trout — The flesh of rainbow trout can be light beige, pink or yellow. It has a strong fish flavor but is delicate when filleted. Good for frying, grilling, baking or poaching.

Tuna — A very dark meat fish when in the raw state, but lightens up when cooked and very flaky. Very good grilled or sautéed.

Turbot — A snowy white meat fish that has a strong fish flavor. Best fried or oven-fried.

Walleye Pollock — Not to be confused with walleye pike (which is a game fish). Similar in taste and texture to cod and great at a fish fry.

BASIC SEAFOOD COOKING

The Seafood Counter-Encounter

If you're an avid fisherman, your "catch of the day" is never too small to fillet. But if you're like most, the question before you is this — "What do I do with this fish?" Most importantly, keep the fish cold (in water or on ice) so it will not spoil. Some people freeze it whole but it's a good idea to gut it first.

GUTTING A FISH:
Wash fish thoroughly. Gut fish by using a very sharp fillet knife. Cut fish lengthwise down the belly from the head to the tail. Open belly cavity and scrape out all the innards. Rinse fish thoroughly again. You may freeze fish in water or wrap in freezer paper with the shiny side of the paper inside.

SCALING A WHOLE FISH:
Using a sharp fillet knife, scale fish by running the knife in short strokes the opposite way of the scales. Keeping the fish moist makes scale removal easy.

FILLETING A WHOLE FISH:
Cut off the head. Run the fillet knife along the backbone lengthwise. Turn the fish over and

repeat. You should have two long pieces of fish meat when finished. If this is confusing to you, don't be afraid to ask a good seafood clerk or fisherman to show you. It's very easy after you've done it once or twice.

BONING A FISH FILLET:
After you have filleted the fish, there will still be side bones. Lay the fillet (skin down) on a cutting surface and using your fillet knife, put the knife under the set of bones and carefully lift and cut trying to leave as much fish intact as you can.

STEAKING A WHOLE FISH:
This process is pretty easy because there is no filleting or boning involved. All you do is lay the whole fish on a flat surface and chop it into steaks (right through the bone). This is called the cross-cut of the fish. Usually an inch thick is about right and this type of cut is very suitable for grilling.

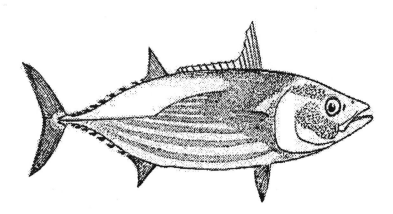

COOKING TIME

When cooking fish — timing is very important to avoid undercooking or overcooking.

Time allowed depends on the thickness of the fish, whether it's whole, filleted or steaked. Allow 10 minutes per inch, measuring at the thickest part of the fish.

If microwaving, cut cooking time down to 2 minutes per inch. And always remember to check fish for flakiness. This holds true for most fish but there are some exceptions. For instance, all shellfish, shark and monkfish will not flake. Their texture is that of meat and will turn opaque when done.

Most fish fillets come skinned when you buy them, but if it has a thin skin on one side, it can be cooked with the skin on and is edible. However, some fish have a very tough skin, such as salmon, shark, tuna and swordfish and halibut. I don't recommend eating the skin. You can still cook it with the skin on though. When cooking is completed, skin will smoothly separate from the fish.

Tip: If you have a fish fillet that is thick at one end and thin at the other, fold the thin end underneath giving the fish an even thickness.

You can do anything with fish if you just pick your favorite method of cooking, whether it be microwaving, grilling, steaming, baking, poaching, broiling, sautéing, frying or oven-frying.

Microwave if you're looking for a quick dinner. Grilling is for all you campers and backyard chefs. Steam or poach for all the careful diet watchers. Bake, broil, fry or oven-fry for the rest of us.

Questions and Answers

Q. How much fish serves one person?
A. 12 oz. whole
6-8 oz. fish fillet

Q. How can I tell if fish is done?
A. Fish will flake easily with a fork. (Exception: shellfish, shark and monkfish are done when opaque.)

Q. How long can I keep fresh fish refrigerated?
A. Fresh fish should be eaten the day it is purchased. If storing it in the refrigerator overnight, be sure to pack your fish in ice. Use a zip lock bag. Place fish inside. Close. Place bag in bowl, surrounded by ice.

Q. How long can I keep frozen fish?
A. Usually no longer than two months. Be sure to use the proper freezer wrap. White freezer paper works very well.

Q. How do I thaw fish?
A. Some say at room temperature for two hours but I would recommend thawing fish in the refrigerator overnight. Thaw shellfish overnight as well but in water.

Q. How can I keep fish from sticking to the grill or pan?
A. Spray pan or grill with a non-stick coating first.

Q. How can I keep the fish odor out of the house?
A. Use tasty spices — garlic, onion, cajun spice, lemon-pepper, basil, Italian seasonings, etc.

Q. What side dishes do I serve with fish?
A. Most anything goes well with fish, but my favorites are: baked beans, cole slaw, macaroni and cheese and hush puppies.

Q. How often should I eat fish?
A. Everyday, if you like, or at least twice a week. Fish is low in fat and cholesterol and high in protein. The best fish to eat because of its high omega 3 oil content is Salmon. Tuna, Mackerel and Sardines are also recommended.

Q. How can I tell if my fish is bad?
A. If it has a very strong odor or feels sticky — it's bad. Just let your nose be the judge. A whole fish should be plump and firm with clear eyes.

Q. How do I tell if my fish is freezer-burned?
A. It will have a discolored look and grainy texture and will feel very light. Also, it will float when placed in water.

Basic Seafood Cooking

Use your favorite fish fillet for any of the following methods of cooking.

BAKING

1. Preheat oven to 400°.
2. Spray non-stick coating on baking dish.
3. Arrange fillets on baking dish.
4. Brush with 1 tablespoon margarine and lemon.
5. Bake for 20 minutes (without turning).
6. Fish is done when it flakes easily with a fork.

MICROWAVING

1. Spray non-stick coating on microwave safe glass dish.
2. Arrange fillets on baking dish.
3. Brush with 1 tablespoon margarine and lemon.
4. Cover with wax paper or saran wrap.

5. Microwave on high, 2 minutes per fillet (do not turn).
6. Fish is done when it flakes easily with a fork.

BROILING

1. Spray broiler pan with non-stick coating.
2. Arrange fillets on broiler pan rack.
3. Brush with 1 tablespoon margarine and lemon.
4. Broil 5 minutes per side or until fish flakes easily with a fork.

SAUTÉING

1. Melt 1 tablespoon margarine in skillet.
2. Arrange fillets in skillet, squeezing fresh lemon over fillets.
3. Sauté over medium heat, approximately 10 minutes per side or until fish flakes easily with a fork.

FRYING

1. Pour 2 cups of oil into a skillet or deep fryer and heat until boiling.
2. Wet fillet and dip into seasoned breadcrumbs.
3. Drop fillet into hot oil (to cover fish).
4. Continue frying until fish turns a golden brown and is flaky when tested with a fork.

OVEN-FRYING

1. Preheat oven to 400°.
2. Spray baking dish with non-stick coating.
3. Coat your fillet with seasoned bread crumbs, breading or corn meal.
4. Arrange fillets in pan.
5. Bake for 20-30 minutes. Do not turn fish.
6. Check fish for flakiness.

POACHING

1. Fill skillet half way with water. (Chicken broth may be used as well.)
2. After water is just about to boil, put in fillets.
3. Simmer until fish flakes easily with a fork.

GRILLING

1. Spray rack with non-stick coating.
2. Place fillets on grill. (Use indirect heat if using a gas grill.)
3. Baste with margarine and lemon.
4. Grill 3-5 minutes per side.
5. Fish is done when it's flaky.

STEAMING

A steamer is a good investment as the kettle can be used as any stock pot and the fitted strainer permits the lid to fit closely maximizing the nutritional value of the food.

1. Pour 1 cup water into large pot and boil.
2. Place colander into pot. (Fish should be *above* not *in* water.)
3. Put fillets into colander and cover.
4. Continue cooking until fish is tender and flaky.

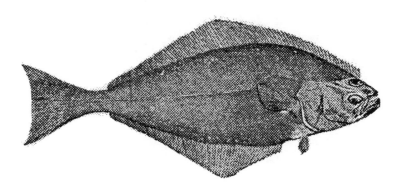

Methods for Cooking Fish

Now I will list the different methods for cooking fish and include one recipe for each. You can then apply your favorite fish to that recipe. For instance, for orange roughy, you could substitute any whitefish, such as: sole, turbot, flounder, cod, halibut, etc. It just depends on what you like best.

Baking

Baked Cod

2	8 oz. cod fillets
1	tablespoon Margarine
1	fresh lemon
¼	cup seasoned breadcrumbs
¼	teaspoon paprika
¼	cup grated cheddar cheese
¼	cup bacon bits

Preheat oven to 400°. Coat baking pan with non-stick coating. Place fillets in pan and brush with margarine. Squeeze on fresh lemon and season with garlic and pepper. Top with seasoned breadcrumbs and bacon bits. Bake for 20 minutes, without turning. Sprinkle on cheddar cheese during last 2 minutes and paprika. To be sure it's done check fish for flakiness.

Serves 2
Serve with: Asparagus and sweet potatoes. Makes a colorful, appetizing dish.

Broiling

Broiled Halibut Steaks

2 8 oz. halibut steaks
1 tablespoon margarine
1 fresh lemon
¼ teaspoon garlic powder
¼ teaspoon basil

Line broiler pan with foil (this saves a messy clean-up). Spray pan rack with a non-stick coating. Place steaks on rack. Brush with melted margarine. Squeeze on fresh lemon. Season with garlic and basil. Broil 5 to 6 minutes per side, occasionally basting (this eliminates dryness). Fish is done when it flakes easily.

Serves 2
Serve with: Buttered carrots and twice-baked potatoes.

Grilling

Grilled Swordfish Steaks

2   8 oz. swordfish steaks
¼   cup teriyaki sauce
½   teaspoon garlic powder
1   tablespoon margarine

Marinate fish 15 minutes per side in teriyaki sauce. Spray grill with a non-stick coating. Grill fish over medium coals 5-6 minutes per side, basting frequently with melted margarine. Season with garlic powder. Check fish for flakiness.

Serves 2
Serve with: Sweet corn and baked beans and a crisp green salad.

Frying

Fried Ocean Perch

1   lb. ocean perch fillets
1   cup Fish Fry Meal or Corn Meal
2   cups oil

Heat oil until boiling. Wet fish and roll in breading. Dip into hot oil to cover fish. A deep-fat fryer basket helps. Fry until fish is golden brown and flakes easily with a fork. Drain on paper towels.

Serves 2
This makes a great fish sandwich. Top with sliced tomato, onion and tartar sauce.

Oven-Frying

Oven-Fried Red Snapper

2   8 oz. fillets Red Snapper
1   tablespoon oil
½ cup seasoned breadcrumbs
½ teaspoon paprika
½ teaspoon garlic
    fresh lemon

Preheat oven to 400°. Oil bottom of baking dish very lightly. Wet fillets. Roll in combined dry ingredients above. Place in baking dish. Squeeze on fresh lemon. Bake 20-30 minutes without turning. Fish is done when flaky.

Serves 2
Serve with: Tartar sauce, whipped potatoes and broccoli.

Sautéing

Sautéed Catfish Fillets

2 8 oz. Catfish Fillets
1 tablespoon margarine
   fresh lemon
½ cup parmesan cheese
½ cup seafood breading
¼ teaspoon paprika
½ cup chopped green pepper
½ cup chopped white onion

Melt margarine in skillet on very low heat. Sauté green pepper and onion until half done. Combine parmesan cheese and breading. Wet fish and roll in dry ingredients. Add to skillet. Sauté on low — 15 minutes per side. Sprinkle on paprika and fresh lemon. Check fish for flakiness to be sure that it's done.

Serves 2
Serve with: Green beans and corn.

Poaching

Poached Salmon Steaks

2   8 oz. salmon steaks
$\frac{1}{2}$ cup water (or chicken broth)
1   tablespoon lemon juice
$\frac{1}{4}$ cup chopped green onion

In skillet, combine water, lemon juice and onion. Heat until just boiling. Add fish. Cover. Lower heat to simmer. Cook 5-6 minutes per side. Salmon will be light pink all the way through and will flake easily with a fork when done.

Serves 2
Serve with: Breaded tomatoes and noodles.

Microwaving

Microwaved Sole Fillets

2   8 oz. sole fillets
2   tablespoons mayonnaise
¼   cup seasoned breadcrumbs
¼   teaspoon paprika
    fresh lemon

Spray bottom of a microwave-safe baking dish with a non-stick coating. Place fillets in baking dish. Spread mayonnaise on fish. Sprinkle breadcrumbs with paprika on top of fish and squeeze on fresh lemon. Cover with waxed paper. Microwave on high 2 minutes for each fillet. Do not turn fish over. Check for flakiness to tell if fish is done.

Serves 2
Serve with: Spanish rice and broccoli.

Steaming

Steamed Orange Roughy

2   8 oz. orange roughy fillets
½ cup water
   Your favorite fresh vegetables such as:
      Carrots
      Broccoli
      Cauliflower
      Asparagus

Use a large pot. Add water and heat until boiling. Place colander in pot. Add fish and vegetables. Cover. Cook above, not in, water approximately 15 minutes. Check fish for flakiness for doneness.

Serves 2
Serve with: Hollandaise sauce or cheese sauce over fish and veggies.

All of the previously mentioned methods are very basic recipes showing you the various ways of cooking the same kind of fish.

Now you are ready to add your favorite seasonings, in addition to the basic margarine and lemon. For example, let's start with orange roughy. Bake it, but in addition to the margarine and lemon, how about sprinkling on a dash of paprika, garlic, one tablespoon breadcrumbs and one tablespoon parmesan cheese. See how easily you added flavor to your fish? Or why not sprinkle on one tablespoon parsley and top with one tablespoon almonds and bacon bits? The next time, pour on a can of stewed tomatoes and top with one tablespoon parmesan cheese.

You don't need an extensive cookbook to show you what a great cook you can be. The best cooks in the world are the ones who are not afraid to experiment. That's what makes cooking fish exciting and fun.

If you're grilling orange roughy, put foil down on the grill first. Spray the foil. Then sauté green peppers and onions until they are half done and place fish right on the veggies. Grill 5 minutes, then turn the fish and grill another 5 minutes. When you put the fish on the plate, pour the peppers and onions over the fish. You'll have the neighbors wondering where that great aroma is coming from. They won't know you're cooking fish.

Now let's talk to all of you who love to go camping. Get your fish ready for the grill before you leave by wrapping each fillet in foil that you have sprayed, dot with margarine and lemon. Top with one tablespoon chopped green pepper, onions, and mushrooms and season with a dash of garlic. Now seal it up with another piece of foil before you put it in your cooler. Grill fish package 10 minutes per side and eat right out of the foil. No messy clean-up. This is also a good one to get ready ahead of time when having company. You can even make the foil in the shape of a fish. Kids love it!

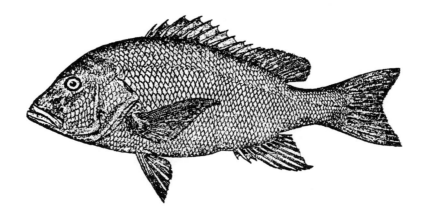

Spices and Marinades

Here's where your creativity comes in. If you check your pantry I'll bet you'll find many of these on hand and many stores carry bottled marinades. You can become a great fish cook. Just use your imagination.

Spices

Bay	Ginger	Papika
Basil	Lemon pepper	Parsley
Cajun spice	Italian seasoning	Rosemary
Dill	Marjoram	Tarragon
Garlic	Oregano	Thyme

Marinades

Butter herb sauce
Dill sauce
Italian Dressing
Mayonnaise
Orange-honey marinade
Orange wine cooler

Seafood Cajun BBQ Sauce
Soy Sauce
Stewed tomatoes
Teriyaki marinade
Teriyaki sauce

Fish is so simple to cook. But if you think you're still not ready to try fish, here's the easiest of all—seafood cooking bags. You use cooking bags for roasts. They have them for fish too! Just place your fish fillet in the cooking bag and bake it according to the directions on the package. Talk about easy. It's the easiest!

My Favorite Fish & Shrimp Breading

Do you ever wonder when you're frying fish or shrimp why your breading falls off? The answer is because the dry breading really has nothing to adhere to. So always use a wet batter first and then roll your fish or shrimp in the dry breading. Seafood breading mix can usually be found at the Seafood shop or the Deli at most supermarkets. If not, substitute any breading mix. You'll have the best fried fish or shrimp around and everyone will want your recipe. Remember — dip your fish or shrimp in very hot oil after breading it and fry it until it's golden brown.

Batter

Fish'N'Chips Batter Mix: Mix with water until it's a pancake consistency.

Breading

1   cup flour
1   package dry seafood breading mix
Season with pepper and garlic.

NOTE: Always drain your fish on paper towels.

Fish 'N' Chips

I recently asked a friend how her fish cooking was coming along. "I'm still baking Orange Roughy rolled in crushed potato chips," she said, "and my husband is kinda bored with it, so I'm changing my recipe. Next time I'm using BBQ chips, then sour cream and onion, then sour cream and chives, maybe crushed taco chips." OK, OK, Patty, that's enough!

Now, she was not afraid to experiment. And that's what I want you to do. The varieties are endless. You'll be finding that you can't wait to try a new recipe.

Potato Chips Recipe

Your favorite fish fillet. Brush with milk. Roll in crushed potato chips. Bake in a 400° oven approximately 20 min. Check for flakiness for doneness. You do not need to turn fish.

Holiday Entertaining

A SHRIMP TRAY

I believe in making party cooking—

    easy and economical
    appetizing
    simple and succulent

Buy your shrimp raw and peel and cook it yourself. You'll save three times what cooked shrimp costs in the stores. If you're thinking about saving time, peel and devein your shrimp and then freeze them raw. When you're ready to boil them, drop them into boiling water (still frozen). They're done when the water comes to the second boil.

A beautiful shrimp tray is so easy to make. Take a platter and cover it with crispy green kale or leafy lettuce. A cup of cocktail sauce should be placed in the center. Arrange your cooked shrimp in a circular pattern and garnish the tray with lemon twists or slices and cherry tomatoes. This looks very appetizing and you have saved money by doing it yourself.

You can add crab or lobster chunks to the tray. They too are delicious dipped in cocktail sauce! A shrimp tray makes a beautiful centerpiece all by itself.

HOW MUCH SHOULD I BUY?

There's never really a set rule. The shrimp is usually the first thing eaten when you're having a party, but here's my general rule of thumb;

BOILED SHRIMP — 6-10 per person (depending on the size of the shrimp, NOT THE PERSON!)

FRIED SHRIMP — 8 Jumbo
                        12 Medium

Here's a tip for making your shrimp go a longer way at a party. Don't spend hours cleaning and deveining it, (most people will eat it like popcorn.) Cook your shrimp in the shell and at an informal gathering, put shrimp and sauce in the middle of the table and let everyone sit around and peel 'n' eat! It's so much fun to do it that way. We have my whole family on videotape, just having a ball!

PEEL 'N' EAT SHRIMP

Allow 1/2 pound per person
Drop shrimp (still in shell) into boiling water. Allow water to come to the second boil and boil shrimp for 1/2 minute for medium size shrimp and 1 minute for jumbo size shrimp. Drain and chill. Serve with cocktail sauce and lemon wedges.

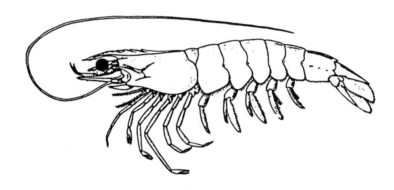

SHRIMP COUNT

Do you know what a tag like this means?

JUMBO RAW SHRIMP
21-25 Count

This tells you how many shrimp are in a pound. Some typical sizes are:

60-70
36-40
40-50
26-30
21-25
Under 10 to the pound

The more shrimp to the pound, the smaller the shrimp.

Many people think that raw shrimp should be light pink to be fresh. This is wrong! Shrimp like people — come in many colors: Brown, white, black, pink and blue (although I don't know any blue people.) Their shell color depends on what part of the world they're from. After you boil your shrimp — any color will turn bright pink.

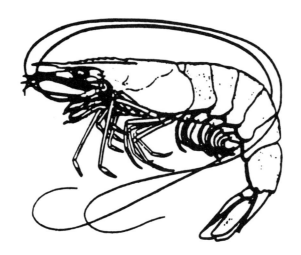

DOS AND DON'TS OF SHRIMP

1. Always buy the freshest shrimp. If the meat looks yellow or the shrimp feels sticky — it is not good. Always pack shrimp in ice. Place the shrimp in a protective zip-lock bag and then place bag in a bowl of ice. Shrimp will stay fresh for up to two days.

2. Never cook shrimp and then freeze. This will cause the shrimp to be tough. When freezing shrimp in the shells, freeze them in a container of water. If cleaning shrimp and freezing them raw, make sure you use freezer paper. Shrimp will stay frozen for several months.

3. Don't overcook shrimp. When the translucent look is gone from the shrimp — IT'S DONE.

4. Don't boil the shrimp before deep frying. Raw shrimp should be peeled and deveined before being dipped in batter and then in hot oil.

Shrimp Recipes

Boiled Shrimp

Peel and devein shrimp. Drop into salted boiling water. Let water come to a second boil. Boil for approximately one minute. Drain and let stand in icy cold water until cooled. Serve with cocktail sauce.

Fried Shrimp

Peel and devein shrimp. Dip into seafood batter lightly. Cook in boiling oil until shrimp is golden brown. Drain shrimp on paper towels. Serve with cocktail sauce and lemon wedges.

Shrimp Scampi

Peel and devein shrimp. Melt margarine in skillet. Add $\frac{1}{2}$ teaspoon parsley flakes. Add $\frac{1}{4}$ teaspoon garlic (crushed). Add shrimp to above mixture and cook slowly until shine is gone from shrimp and they turn a bright pink in color. Serve shrimp over rice.

A SHRIMP TREE

You didn't know shrimp grew on trees?
Well — Anything is possible at holiday time! Let's make one!

You'll need one 12-inch styrofoam cone and a package of frilled toothpicks.

1   lb. boiled jumbo shrimp
1   large green pepper (uncooked and cubed)
8   oz. cocktail sauce
2   (8 oz.) cream cheese — softened
½   lb. crab chunks
½   lb. lobster chunks
1   cup pineapple chunks
    Leafy green lettuce or kale (enough to cover cone)

Cover styrofoam cone with lettuce or kale. Set aside.

Take a large tray and put crab dip (see recipe on page 53) in center — making a well. Place cone in well using dip to anchor cone to tray.

TO DECORATE TREE:

Secure shrimp, lobster, crab, peppers and pineapple to tree using toothpicks (frilled or colored). Completely cover tree.
Surround tree and dip with crackers and have a cup of cocktail sauce to the side for dipping.

Note: To keep the seafood on the tree cold, spray it occasionally with ice water.

HAPPY HOLIDAYS!

COCKTAIL SAUCE

This recipe is my favorite homemade cocktail sauce. If it's too spicy for your taste, add extra ketchup. If it's not spicy enough, add extra horseradish. And if you have any left-over sauce when the shrimp is gone — use it in your next batch of meat loaf instead of just plain ketchup. It'll give it some zip! I hope you like it.

1   cup ketchup
1   tablespoon horseradish
1   tablespoon chili sauce
1   teaspoon lemon juice
This is enough for one pound of shrimp.

CRAB DIP

½ lb. crab (real and blend) flaked
1 pkg. (8 oz.) softened cream cheese
½ cup chopped green onion
½ cup cocktail sauce

Mix above ingredients together and stir until creamy.

Note: Crab or lobster blend is a combination of crab or lobster and pollock, a whitefish. It is fully cooked and can be used at less cost than crab or lobster.

LOBSTER

ARE YOU STILL WITH ME? I hope so, because you're now ready for LOBSTER!

Imagine that you're dining out for your anniversary or some other special occasion. The menu is filled with tantalizing seafood. The one most enjoyed by all is lobster.

So you order the lobster and when the waiter brings it to you, you think how great it would be if you could prepare it right in your own kitchen once in a while.

Well, you can! And probably for half the cost. Don't be intimidated — it's really simple. You just have to know how to do it!

So let's start with some questions and answers.

Q. How much lobster will serve one?
A. 8-10 oz. tail is adequate.

Q. What's the difference between cold water and warm water lobster?
A. Cold water tails are from the frigid waters off the New England coast. They are firmer and sweeter than warm water tails, which are from Central America and Florida.

Q. What are the methods for cooking lobster?
A. Boil, Broil, Grill or French-Fry.

Q. How can I tell when my lobster tail is done?
A. The Lobster meat will turn opaque (a bright white, and the translucent look will be gone.)

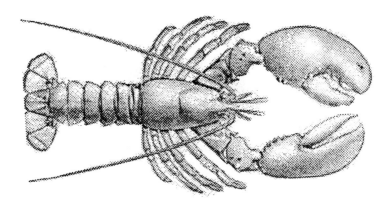

SPLITTING A LOBSTER TAIL

To Broil, Grill or French Fry a lobster tail;

Split the shell open. Start by completely thawing out the tail (see page 21). Lay tail on a flat surface with shell side up. Hold sharp knife with blade on middle of the shell with one hand and use heel of the other hand to hit down on the blade back (cracking the shell). This avoids contact with the sharp side of the knife.

Now that the shell is cracked, use index finger to separate lobster meat from the shell. Run finger between shell and meat until shell is loosened. Fold shell underneath and spread lobster meat over shell.

It's easy — just go slowly. But if you're still uncertain, a good seafood shop clerk will probably be happy to do it for you. Just call ahead and ask them to thaw and split the shell for you. Or, you might even want to watch so you'll know how to do it the next time.

BOILED LOBSTER TAIL

Drop an 8-10 oz. tail into enough boiling water seasoned with crab boil to cover. (Crab boil is a combination of herbs and bay leaf). It can be purchased ready-made at your favorite seafood shop, and if it's bagged (like tea bags) after one use drain and keep in freezer for another time.

Let the water come back to the second boil and boil for 6-8 minutes.

Melt butter. Allow salt to settle. Pour off oil. (This is "drawn butter.")

Serve with drawn butter and lemon wedges.

BROILED LOBSTER TAIL

Thaw lobster tail and split the shell open, exposing the meat. Brush with butter and broil until the meat turns opaque all the way through to the middle. Baste with butter several times while broiling. Sprinkle on paprika and serve with drawn butter in small hot cups and lemon wedges.

GRILLED LOBSTER TAIL

Thaw and split the shell. Grill over medium hot coals, open side down for 1-2 minutes. Finish grilling with flat side on grill and top shell open (keeping lid closed). Frequently baste with butter. Grill until meat turns opaque and sprinkle paprika on top during last minute of cooking.

Serve with drawn butter and lemon wedges.

FRENCH-FRIED LOBSTER TAIL

Remove lobster meat completely from shell.
Dip meat into seafood batter and drain.
Drop lobster meat into boiling oil and cook until lobster turns golden brown and will float to the top.
Drain on paper towels.

LIVE LOBSTER

Don't let a live lobster hold your hand, because he might not let go!

Playfully, I once placed a pencil between a lobster's claw just to see what he would do. He snapped it right in half! This is why you see the rubberbands on lobster claws.

To purchase a live lobster, remember the following:

1. 1 lb. to $1\frac{1}{2}$ lb. serves one person.
2. Buy a lobster that is lively.
3. Store in refrigerator until ready to cook.
4. Cook a live lobster the same day you purchase it.
5. Storing live lobster in water in refrigerator will kill it instantly. Keep lobster in box or bag in refrigerator until ready to cook or put it in the freezer. Two hours should be sufficient to assure a more humane way of preparing the lobster for its boiling water plunge!

COOKING A LIVE LOBSTER

Use a large pot (fill $\frac{3}{4}$ with water).
Drop lobster into boiling water (Head first).
Lobster will immediately turn bright red, so make sure lobster is completely submerged.

A medium size lobster (1 to $1\frac{1}{2}$ lbs.) takes approximately 6-8 minutes to cook after water comes to the second boil.

HOW TO EAT A MAINE LOBSTER

1. Twist off claws.
2. Crack each claw with a nutcracker (the meat in the claws is very sweet).
3. Separate the tail from the body by arching the back and twisting off the tail.
4. Break off the flipper at the end of the tail.
5. Insert a fork where the flippers were and push meat out.
6. The small claws are good too — just snip off one end and suck like a straw.

POOR MAN'S LOBSTER: MONKFISH

The monkfish has a large head, tiny eyes and a huge tooth-filled mouth.

Its body is flat and thin and it can weigh as much as fifty pounds.

It is caught in the Western Atlantic Ocean. Its flesh is firm, white and has the consistency of lobster meat (but not quite as sweet).

The tail is the only edible part of the monkfish.

Boil, Broil, Grill, or French-Fry. Cook just like lobster.

For recipes see pages 92 and 93.

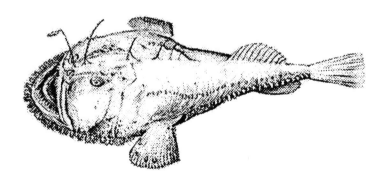

FOR SERIOUS DIETERS

Diet This and Diet That

Diets are so overwhelming these days. There are:

Diet Pills
Diet Drinks
Diet Tapes
Diet Books
Diet Gimmicks
Diet Clubs
Diet through Hypnosis
Diet Patches

and then there is SEAFOOD, plain and simple. And it's good for you.

However you cut fat, cuts fat off you.

For 20 years I cooked whatever we liked. Fried food or fatty foods. I am now trying to change my cooking style without shocking my family.

The Fishlady is going to show you a healthy eating plan. These are not drastic changes. It's just to help you be wise about what you buy and cook. These are all health-giving choices.

Start out with little changes that others will barely notice. Only you will know.

Try: Skim milk for whole milk (especially in cooking)
    Lean meat for fat meat
    Low fat cottage cheese for cream cheese
    Clear broth soup for creamed soups
    Fresh fruit for canned or sugared fruit
    Whole grain bread for white bread
    Whole grain flour for white flour
    Angelfood cake for regular cake mixes
    Natural meat juice for creamed gravy
    Oven-fried fish for deep fried fish
    Ice milk or sherbet for ice cream

Fruit juices for soda pop
Fresh steamed veggies for canned veggies
Baked potatoes for mashed or fried
Egg whites or egg substitutes for whole egg with yolk

Nobody likes fish for all three meals — especially not for breakfast. At least Americans don't. I don't know why, but even the Fishlady doesn't want fish for breakfast. So that leaves lunch and dinner. Salads are light and good for lunch, so try tossing in a little crab or popcorn shrimp. How about an omelet filled with veggies and crab. (If using two eggs, to cut down on cholesterol, use only one yolk.) These are just two simple ideas to get you started.

Snacks were always my downfall. That candy bar at three o'clock will surely hold me 'til dinner. Well, they're not very nutritional, and are loaded with calories. Instead of that candy bar, have a crabstick and maybe even a little cocktail sauce to go with it. Make sure it's low-cal cocktail sauce. Or dip the crabstick in reduced calorie melted margarine. How about crab dip on a celery stick? Who said diets have to be boring! <u>Just eat the right stuff.</u>

You could eat fish every evening for dinner. It's so versatile. There are hundreds of varieties and many different ways to cook fish. There's even a fish that tastes like chicken.

Just the Facts

Q. What is a calorie?
A. A calorie is a unit for measuring the energy produced by food when oxidized in the body.

Q. What is protein?
A. Protein is a basic nutrient of all living cells, from amoebas to human beings. Protein is the essential building block for all our tissues, bones, internal organs, glands, nervous system, blood, skin, teeth and even fingernails.

Protein is animal in origin. It is found in meats, fowl, dairy products and fish.

Q. What is a carbohydrate?
A. A carbohydrate performs the function of providing lasting energy for the body and for any sort of muscular exertion.

Carbohydrates are found in grains, vegetables and fruits.

Q. What is fat?
A. Fat is found in meat, cream, oils or oily foods. Fat is what none of us wants to be, so eat foods rich in natural nutrients. They will seldom add a pound.

Q. What is a good diet?
A. A good diet consists of:

> adequate protein
> moderate fat
> moderate carbohydrates
> addition of polyunsaturated oils

Q. What's the difference in saturated and polyunsaturated?
A. Saturated oil is generally a fat of animal origin. These are oils to stay away from because they harden in your body. Examples are: butter, lard, chicken fat, palm oil, coconut oil and plant oil. Polyunsaturated oils are: olive oil, canola (from rape seed) safflower, soybean, sunflower, corn, cottonseed and sesame. They lower blood cholesterol.

REMEMBER: The more saturated, the harder the fat, the more it clogs the arteries.

We do need proteins, but not the large quantities that most of us consume. For a time, we were told that high protein, low carbohydrate diets were best. Now, the research done by Johns Hopkins Medical School and others has determined that we do of course need protein but in better balance with carbohydrates. The New England Journal of Medicine has published similar findings by other medical institutions.

Also, proteins are found not just in animal products but also in certain plants. A serving of rice and beans provides an adequate amount of protein.

Complex carbohydrates are as essential as protein and are found in carrots, broccoli, sprouts, squash, sweet potatoes and cauliflower.

Q. What is cholesterol?
A. Cholesterol is a substance that tends to build up in the blood vessels and clog them. Cholesterol is a normal constituent of blood and tissues and is found in every animal cell. Some cholesterol is generated by the body itself — chiefly by the liver — the rest is supplied by your diet.

Please see pages 189 and 190 for a calorie/cholesterol/fat chart.

Q. What foods should I avoid while dieting or just wanting to feel healthier?
A. Here's my list:

Fried fish or meat	Pizza
Casseroles	Bacon
Sausage	Whole milk
Cream soup	Cheese dressing
Creamed vegetables	Fried vegetables
Gravy	Butter
Cheese	Sour cream
Pie	Cake
Ice Cream	Pudding

Q. What are some low fat condiments?
A. Lemons
Limes
Flavored vinegars
Horseradish
Tomato salsa
Vinaigrettes
Oil-free dressings
Reduced sodium soy sauce

Q. What's a good marinade for fish?
A. Skim milk instead of oil based marinades, any kind of citrus juice, or even wine coolers. (The alcohol content evaporates during cooking.)

Q. What are the benefits of shellfish?
A. Although shellfish is high in cholesterol, it is low in saturated fat and loaded with Omega 3.

Q. What is Omega 3?
A. Omega 3 is a polyunsaturated fatty acid found in high concentrations in certain saltwater fish, such as mackerel, salmon, tuna, sardines and shellfish. Omega 3 fish oils rid the body of certain cholesterols. It is essential for good vision and normal brain development.

Q. Why do we need fish oil?
A. Fish oil may lower the risk of many diseases, such as heart disease, arthritis and psoriasis.

Seafood
Part of a Healthy Way of Life

Fish and the Eskimos

The Eskimo diet is high in marine fish containing Omega 3 and Eskimos rarely have heart attacks.

FACT:

In Greenland between 1954 and 1970, only three heart attacks were reported in a population of 1800 people. Eskimos eat marine rather than animal fat.

Salmon and Arteries

FACT:

Salmon is loaded with fish oil and helps clean out the plaque build-up in one's arteries.

Fish and Pasta

There are many types of pasta and those made up of whole grain or unbleached flour contain complex carbohydrates. Regular pasta is nutritious — not fattening, except for the ingredients that make up the sauces we use.

You know the different methods to prepare the same fish, but I'll list them once again, so you don't have to backtrack.

Baking
Broiling
Microwaving
Poaching
Steaming
Grilling or Sautéing
Oven-Frying
and
Frying

The last one is really the only method of seafood cooking you need to avoid if you're watching your weight and cholesterol. Oven-fry instead.

Fish 'n' Quick

Everyone is busy. None of us seems to have time for a balanced, nutritious dinner. Right? Wrong, if you have a microwave.

Don't make dinner a grab bag: grab this, and grab that. You can prepare this next meal in 10 minutes.

Here's your 10-minute Fish 'n' Quick meal:

1. Microwave a baked potato (usually about 5 minutes).

2. Microwave a fish fillet (usually about 2 minutes).

3. Microwave your favorite vegetables (about 3 minutes).

Is that fast? And it's low calorie and balanced.

The Best Way

For dieting, or just deciding to eat healthier dinners, the best way to prepare fish is by steaming. That locks in all the vitamins and nutrients and it's very easy to prepare.

A steamer is good but a large pot with a lid, and a colander, works very well. Add some fresh vegetables such as broccoli, carrots or cauliflower. Cook fish and veggies until the fish is flaky and the veggies are tender. What a delicious, low-cal dinner! Squeeze lemon or lime juice over fish and veggies.

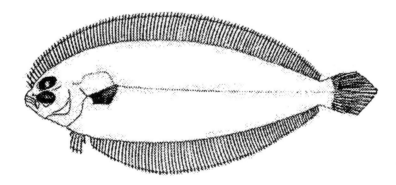

Oven-frying

Oven-frying fish is like deep-frying, except for one thing. Instead of submerging the fish in hot oil, bake it in the oven — a very hot oven. Wet your fish and roll it in breading, as if to deep fry. Preheat oven to 400°, spray baking dish with nonstick cooking spray or coat lightly with canola or corn oil and bake fish for 20 minutes (uncovered and do not turn). It is as easy as cooking fishsticks and a lot fewer calories.

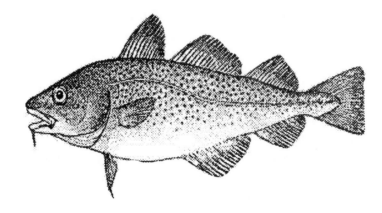

Chicken That Doesn't Cluck

One of our newest varieties of fish is called pomfret. Most seafood shops carry it frozen, since it comes from the Indian Ocean. Pomfret is a very large fish and is also called angelfish. The flesh is like chicken in color and texture and can be prepared like chicken. Cut up in a stir-fry or chicken noodle soup, but call it fish noodle soup or seafood noodle soup!

A friend told me a story about her young son. She likes her boys to eat fish so one evening she cooked some pomfret — not telling them it was fish. Later that evening, someone asked her son what he had for dinner and he said "chicken and french fries." What could give you a more accurate description of the taste?

FISH RECIPE

Any kind of fish (1 lb. filleted)
1   6 oz. can orange juice concentrate

Preheat oven to 350°.

Arrange fillets in baking dish.

Spread on orange juice concentrate.

Bake for 20-25 minutes or until fish is flaky.

Serves 2
Serve with: Asparagus and corn.

A School of Fish

We all have an obligation to our children — the new generation. They learn so much from us. Let's teach them about fish; not just fishsticks.

In our weekly meal planning, let's put fish at the top of the list. Fish isn't the greasy, fried food it used to be. There are new, light and mild varieties swimming around in the sea, and so many exciting, appetizing ways to prepare them.

How about a FISH PIZZA? Kids love it for lunch!

Fish Pizza

1 lb. any chunky whitefish such as; halibut or cod
1 large green pepper (sliced into rings)
1 large tomato (sliced)
1 cup parmesan cheese
1 tablespoon oregano

Preheat oven to 400°.

Lay pepper rings on cookie sheet that you have sprayed with a non-stick coating.

Place piece of fish inside ring.

Top with tomato and sprinkle on cheese and oregano.

Bake 20 minutes. Fish is done when it is flaky.

THE FISHLADY'S FAVORITE RECIPES

LOBSTER/CRAB APPETIZERS

You may use crab or lobster blend in any of the following recipes:

LOBSTER SALAD

1   lb. cooked lobster (shredded)
¼   cup chopped pimento
¼   cup chopped celery
8   oz. pkg. frozen uncooked peas
6   chopped hard boiled eggs
1   cup salad dressing or mayo
¼   teaspoon pepper
¼   teaspoon paprika
    Salt to taste

Mix above ingredients together, sprinkling paprika on top.

Chill — Serve on lettuce leaf, with crackers.

LOBSTER FRIES

1   lb. lobster meat
1   pkg. seafood batter mix
4   cups oil

Cut lobster meat into chunks.
Dip into batter mix and then into hot oil.
Fry until they are golden brown.
Drain onto paper towels.

Delicious dipped in hot drawn butter or seafood cocktail sauce.

For a reminder about drawn butter see page 57.

LOBSTER DIP

½ lb. minced lobster meat (cooked)
8 oz. sour cream
8 oz. softened cream cheese
1 tablespoon Worcestershire sauce
¼ cup chopped green onion

Mix above ingredients together until creamy.

Great for a veggie dip!

SWEET 'N' SOUR SAUCE

1   cup sugar
½ cup each white vinegar and water
(Simmer 5 minutes.)

2   teaspoons cornstarch
1   tablespoon cold water
Combine above ingredients and stir over medium heat until thick consistency.

LITTLE LOBSTER PIES

1   large frozen pie crust (thawed)
½   lb. cooked lobster pieces
8   oz. sweet 'n' sour sauce
8   oz. shredded cheddar cheese

Preheat oven to 350°.

Using a small, round cookie cutter, cut out small pieces of dough from the pie crust and arrange on a cookie sheet.

Brush each piece with sweet 'n'sour sauce and top with lobster and cheddar cheese.

Bake for 10-15 minutes.

Serve warm.

LOBSTER PASTA SHELLS

$\frac{1}{2}$ lb. cooked lobster (shredded)
8 oz. pkg. rigatoni noodles (cooked and drained)
1 cup cooked rice
16 oz. jar spaghetti sauce with mushrooms

Preheat oven to 350°.

Mix cooked lobster and rice together and stuff into noodles. Place each noodle in baking dish and pour spaghetti sauce over top.

If desired, sprinkle top with parmesan cheese or shredded mozzarella.

Bake 20 minutes.

Lobster Entrees

LOBSTER QUICHE

1   lb. cooked, shredded lobster meat
8   oz. pkg. frozen asparagus (cooked)
1   (8 inch) frozen pie shell
8   oz. shredded american cheese
1   can cream of mushroom soup (undiluted)
6   eggs (lightly beaten)

Preheat oven to 350°.

Mix above ingredients together and pour into pie shell. Bake until toothpick comes out clean after being inserted into center of pie. (Approximately 20-30 minutes.)

Serves 4

LOBSTER NEWBURG

1   lb. cooked lobster (cut into pieces)
2   tablespoons margarine
1   cup sherry
¼   teaspoon paprika
1   cup cream
    salt and pepper to taste

Lightly simmer lobster in margarine. Add sherry, paprika, salt and pepper. Simmer 2 minutes. Add cream and simmer until slightly thickened.

Serve over toast or in baked pastry shell.

Serves 4

LOBSTER LOAF

3   lbs. lobster (cooked and shredded)
2   eggs
1   cup seasoned breadcrumbs
½ cup chopped green onions
    salt and pepper to taste
½ cup chopped green pepper
2   cups rice (cooked)
½ cup chopped parsley

Preheat oven to 350°.

Mix above ingredients together and form into oblong shape. Place in buttered loaf-baking dish and bake for 20-30 minutes. Sprinkle top with parsley flakes before serving.

This is great served with a cheese sauce on the side for dipping.

Serves 6

CHEESE SAUCE

2   tablespoons margarine
2   tablespoons flour
1   cup milk
½   cup shredded cheddar cheese

Melt margarine in saucepan over low heat. Blend in flour and add milk. Stir until smooth. Add cheese and stir until thickened.

BROILED MONKFISH

1   lb. monkfish
4   tablespoons margarine
Seasonings:
Lemon pepper, paprika, garlic powder, parsley flakes.

Spray grill with a non-stick coating. Monkfish will be thick, so before cooking it, cut fish lengthwise (almost all the way through) and fan open. This is called butterflying. It will now cook faster and more evenly.

Season melted margarine with spices.

Lay fish on grill or broiler and baste with margarine.

It's done when the fish turns opaque.

Serves 2

MONKFISH KABOBS

1   lb. monkfish (cubed)
1   green pepper (uncooked & cubed)
    Enough pineapple chunks and large mushrooms to put on 12 kabobs
    Wooden skewers
12 cherry tomatoes
2   tablespoons soy sauce and reserved pineapple juice

Alternate above ingredients on wooden skewers with cherry tomato in the middle of each kabob.

Marinate kabobs in mixture of pineapple juice and soy sauce for 30 minutes.

Grill for 5-6 minutes per side, basting with pineapple juice and soy sauce.

Serves 4

SHRIMP RECIPES

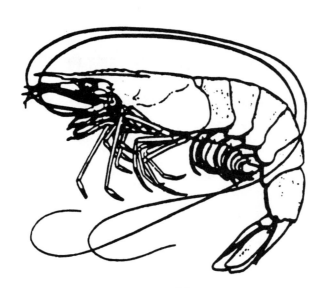

Shrimp Appetizers

SHRIMP SALAD

1   lb. cooked shrimp (cut up)
¼ cup chopped green pepper
⅛ cup chopped pimento
4   chopped hard boiled eggs
⅛ teaspoon pepper or 1 tablespoon paprika
1   cup mayo or salad dressing (optional: 1 tablespoon lemon juice)

Combine above ingredients and sprinkle top with seasoned breadcrumbs and paprika. Chill and serve on a lettuce leaf with crackers or mini party rye.

OR:

Mix above ingredients, sprinkle top with paprika and serve as sandwich or on toasted English muffin or a bagel.

SHRIMP BALL

¼ lb. cooked diced shrimp
2 (8 oz.) cream cheese — softened
¼ teaspoon Worcestershire sauce
1 teaspoon chopped green onion
12 buttery crackers (crushed)

Mix cream cheese, Worcestershire sauce and green onion together.
Add shrimp.
Form into ball.
Roll in crushed buttery crackers.
Chill and serve with crackers or celery sticks.

SHRIMP IN A BLANKET

2 dozen medium raw shrimp (peeled)
1 pkg. unbaked crescent rolls
½ stick melted margarine
¼ teaspoon minced garlic
¼ teaspoon chopped parsley

Preheat oven to 350°.
Parboil shrimp until they just start to curl (drain).
Slice crescent rolls until you have 24 long strips.
Spread with combined margarine, garlic and parsley.
Place one raw shrimp in center of crescent roll and roll it up.
Spread top of roll with margarine mixture.
Bake until rolls are golden brown (approximately 8-10 minutes).

SHRIMP BOAT

$\frac{1}{2}$ lb. shrimp (cooked & chopped)
6   ripe avocados — seed removed
$\frac{3}{4}$ cup mayonnaise
$\frac{1}{4}$ cup chopped green pepper
1   tablespoon lemon juice
$\frac{1}{4}$ cup seasoned breadcrumbs

Mix above ingredients together and stuff into avocados that have been split and brushed with lemon juice (to keep them from turning brown).

SHRIMP HORSESHOE

1   lb. shrimp (cooked and chopped)
12   slices rye bread (cut at angle)
16   oz. jar cheese spread
     Paprika

Preheat oven to 350°.
Place slices of rye bread on cookie sheet.
Place shrimp on rye bread and top with a spoonful of cheese spread.
Sprinkle with paprika.
Bake until cheese is melted (approximately 5 minutes).
Serve warm.

SHRIMP PIZZA

1   lb. shrimp (cooked and cut up)
2   (8 oz.) cream cheese (softened)
8   oz. cocktail sauce
½   cup chopped green onion
1   cup shredded mozzarella cheese

Spread cream cheese on medium size pizza pan.
Spread cocktail sauce on top of cream cheese.
Arrange shrimp on top of cocktail sauce.
Sprinkle on onion and cheese.
Serve with crackers or taco chips and serve this pizza cold.

Shrimp Main Courses

SHRIMP SCAMPI

1   lb. peeled & deveined shrimp (raw)
1   stick melted margarine or butter
1   tablespoon crushed garlic
1   tablespoon chopped parsley (fresh or flakes)
½   teaspoon lemon juice
½   teaspoon paprika
     pepper to taste

Over medium heat, sauté shrimp in above mixture — cooking slowly — until translucent look is gone from shrimp.

NOTE: The above recipe can also be used when cooking scallops. Scallops will turn bright white when cooked. You might even use a little white wine for added flavor.
Serves 4

STUFFED SHRIMP

24 jumbo raw shrimp (peeled)
½ cup milk
1   cup seasoned breadcrumbs
⅛ cup chopped green onions
⅛ cup chopped pimento
¼ cup shredded cheddar & parmesan cheese
1 teaspoon lemon juice
¼ teaspoon crushed garlic
3 tablespoons margarine
4 slices shredded bread

Preheat oven to 350°

Split shrimp and fan open. Dip in milk and roll in breadcrumbs & seasonings. Sauté onion and garlic in margarine. Stir in pimento, lemon juice and shredded bread. Stuff mixture into shrimp and sprinkle with cheese. Bake 20 minutes until shrimp is golden brown. Serve with cheese sauce (page 91).

Serves 4

SHRIMP CASSEROLE

1 lb. peeled and deveined raw shrimp
8 oz. shell macaroni
1 (8 oz.) can cream of celery soup (undiluted)
8 oz. pkg. frozen broccoli
8 oz. pkg. velveeta cheese
½ cup breadcrumbs
1 small can chopped mushroom pieces

Preheat oven to 350°.
Parboil raw shrimp until tails begin to curl (drain).
Cook macaroni in 4 cups boiling water until tender (drain).
Cook broccoli according to direction on package (drain).
Drain canned mushrooms.

Mix the above ingredients together and place in buttered casserole dish. Top with breadcrumbs and bake for 25 minutes.
Serve with crusty french bread and a fresh spinach salad with vinaigrette dressing.

Serves 4

SHRIMP CREOLE

1 lb. raw shrimp (peeled and deveined)
4 tablespoons margarine
1 cup chopped celery
1 cup chopped green pepper
1 cup chopped green onion
1 minced clove garlic
¼ teaspoon cayenne pepper
2 cans whole tomatoes (crushed)
6 cups cooked rice

Melt margarine in skillet. Add green pepper, celery, green onions and garlic and sauté until almost tender. Add cayenne pepper and tomatoes and cook over medium heat for five minutes. Add shrimp and simmer for five minutes or until shrimp are pink.

Serve over cooked rice.

Serves 4

SHRIMP DE JONGHE

1 lb. cleaned, cooked shrimp

1/2 cup margarine

1 tablespoon minced garlic

1 tablespoon parsley flakes

1/2 teaspoon paprika

1/2 cup dry white wine

8 slices dried bread (crumbled)

1/4 cup chopped green onion
   Dash pepper

1/4 cup parmesan cheese

Preheat oven to 350°.
Melt margarine in saucepan on low heat.
Add garlic, parsley, white wine, breadcrumbs, green onion and pepper.
Place shrimp in buttered baking dish and spread buttery mixture on top.
Top with paprika and parmesan cheese.
Bake for 20-25 minutes or until breadcrumbs are browned.
Serve with: Spanish Rice and asparagus.
Serves 4

SWEET 'N' SOUR SHRIMP

1   lb. raw shrimp (peeled and deveined)
1   cup sweet 'n' sour sauce (recipe on page 85)
¼ cup seasoned breadcrumbs
5   cups cooked rice

Simmer shrimp in sweet 'n' sour sauce until shrimp turns pink (approximately 5 minutes). Serve over rice. Top with breadcrumbs.

Serves 4

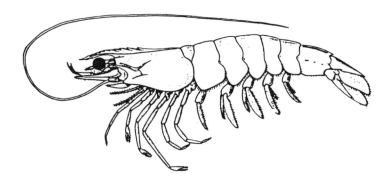

SHRIMP STIR-FRY

1   lb. raw shrimp (peeled and deveined)
16   oz. pkg. frozen chinese vegetables
2   tablespoons teriyaki sauce
1   tablespoon peanut oil
5   cups cooked rice

Sauté veggies in peanut oil.
Add raw shrimp and teriyaki sauce.
Simmer until shrimp turns pink, stirring constantly (approximately 5 minutes).

Serve over rice.

Serves 4

EASY STIR-FRY

1   lb. peeled and deveined raw shrimp
1   tablespoon soy sauce
1   pkg. frozen chinese vegetables
½ cup chunky pineapple

Sauté chinese vegetables in soy sauce. Add raw shrimp and pineapple and simmer, stirring occasionally until shrimp are pink, not translucent.

Serve over cooked rice.

Serves 2

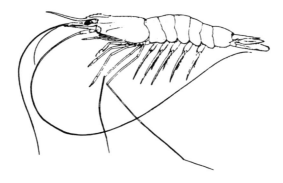

SKEWERED SHRIMP

1   lb. 21/25 count raw shrimp (peeled and deveined)
¼   cup pineapple juice
1   can pineapple chunks
1   large green pepper chunked
6   wooden skewers

Use 10 inch wooden skewers.
Skewer shrimp, pineapple chunks and green pepper.
Grill approximately 5 minutes per side basting frequently with pineapple juice.

SHRIMP AND CORN BOIL

1   lb. 40/50 count raw shrimp (unpeeled)
4   ears sweet corn
1   tablespoon crab boil
1   tablespoon lemon juice
3   qts. boiling water

In a large pot, cook corn until half done (approximately 5 minutes).
Add shrimp, crab boil and lemon juice.
Boil until shrimp turn pink and curl, approximately 3-5 minutes.
Drain, and serve piping hot.

Serves 2

Crab Recipes

SURIMI

Is it crab or lobster?
It's both and more.

Surimi is the name given to cooked crab or lobster combined with pollock. Pollock is a mild whitefish used in many frozen fish products.

Some brands use as much as 1/3 real crab or lobster in the combination, while others use only the crab or lobster juices. Ask for surimi or "fake crab" at the seafood counter. It's also sold in stick form at the deli.

Many restaurants and consumers use crab or lobster surimi in recipes calling for the real thing.

In the following section with recipes calling for lobster or crabmeat, surimi will do just fine at about one-fourth the cost.

As it is precooked you can eat it cold or use it in salads, dips, stews, stir-fries or with pasta.

CRAB PIZZA

1 large pizza pan

Spread pizza pan with two 8 oz. cream cheese (softened). Spread 8 oz. shrimp cocktail sauce over cream cheese. Top with shredded crab-seafood blend. Sprinkle on 4 oz. shredded cheddar cheese. Sprinkle on $\frac{1}{2}$ cup chopped green onion. Pepper and garlic powder to taste. Serve with crackers or taco chips.

CRAB-TACO DIP

$\frac{1}{2}$ pound crab-seafood blend
8   oz. sour cream
8   oz. Taco style cheddar cheese, shredded
8   oz. mild salsa

Season with garlic, pepper, cajun spice or taco spice to taste. Mix above ingredients together and serve on taco chips.

CRAB DIP

½ pound crab-seafood blend
2   8 oz. pkgs. softened cream cheese
4   oz. shrimp cocktail sauce

Mix above ingredients together and serve on crackers or party rye bread.

CRAB CASSEROLE

½ lb. crab-seafood blend
1 7 oz. jar sliced mushrooms
1 pkg. egg noodles
1 can cream of mushroom soup
½ cup shredded cheddar cheese
½ cup breadcrumbs or potato chips

Preheat oven to 350°.

Cook noodles until tender, drain and pour into a casserole dish. Add mushrooms, soup, cheddar cheese and crab-blend. Mix together. Sprinkle breadcrumbs or crushed potato chips over top. Bake for 30 minutes.

CRAB ROLL

$\frac{1}{2}$ lb. crab-seafood blend
2   8 oz. pkgs. softened cream cheese
$\frac{1}{4}$ cup green onion, chopped
$\frac{1}{4}$ cup pecans, chopped

Combine crab, cream cheese and onion. Roll into ball or log. Roll in pecans and chill. Serve with wheat crackers.

CRAB QUICHE

8 inch pastry shell (unbaked)

½ lb. crab-seafood blend

1 dozen raw eggs, beaten lightly

¼ cup green pepper, chopped

¼ cup green onions, chopped

Preheat oven to 350°.

Combine above ingredients and pour into an unbaked pastry shell. Bake for 30-40 minutes or until eggs are cooked, testing with a toothpick in center for doneness.

CRAB SALAD

1   lb. crabmeat or crab blend
6   egg whites (hard boiled and sliced)
¼ cup pimento
⅓ cup sliced black olives
1   tablespoon lemon juice
½ teaspoon black pepper
¼ cup sliced green onions
½ cup vinaigrette dressing (lite)

Mix all of the above ingredients together and chill approximately 1 hour.

Serve on toasted wheat croissant.

ANOTHER CRAB SALAD

1   pound crab-seafood blend
6   hard-boiled eggs, chopped (for less cholesterol, discard yolks of three of the eggs)
½   cup green pepper, chopped
1   cup salad dressing

Season with pepper, garlic, chives and top with paprika. Serve on a leaf of lettuce for a luncheon or as a great side dish or appetizer before your meal.

SOUPS AND STEWS

I hope my section on soups and stews will warm your hearts and souls!

There is nothing like a big pot of stew on a cold winter's night.

The nice part about making a fish stew is that you can use leftovers, too.

Freeze the fish you have left over and when you have accumulated enough make a stew.

Winter Stew

A crock pot works great for this easy stew. Just pour everything in all at once and let it cook all day. Start it on a high setting for an hour and turn it to low for the day.

Ingredients:

1 28 oz. can whole peeled tomatoes
1 large can tomato juice
1 pkg. frozen mixed veggies
macaroni

Seasoning:

1 teaspoon each: garlic, Italian seasoning, parsley, seafood

bouillon cube (or clam juice), pepper, onion, salt

Add:

Chunked fish such as:
Halibut
Cod
Orange Roughy
Or any of your favorite fish. It could even be leftover fish from the night before.
For each cup of fish add a half cup of uncooked macaroni.

Cook stew until it's thick and the fish is flaky.

BOUILLABAISSE

3 teaspoons margarine
1 medium onion (diced)
½ cup green pepper (chopped)
½ cup celery (chopped)
1 clove garlic (minced)
1 bay leaf
½ cup dry white wine
2 tablespoons chopped parsley
1 large can chopped tomatoes
1 (10 oz.) can chicken broth
1 lb. chunky whitefish: cod, snapper, halibut or any fish that you have frozen from leftovers
— also shellfish

Sauté onion, green pepper, celery and garlic in skillet over low heat. Stir in chunked fish and simmer until fish begins to flake. Combine all ingredients in large pot and simmer until piping hot. Sprinkle top with parmesan cheese and serve with crusty french bread or croutons.

Serves 4

CHEESY-CRAB SOUP

½ lb. crab or lobster blend
2 cups milk
1 cup shredded cheddar cheese
1 teaspoon worcestershire sauce
1 teaspoon paprika
3 tablespoons flour

Combine above ingredients and simmer until thickened, stirring frequently.

Serve with hot crescent rolls or breadsticks.

Serves 2

CLAM CHOWDER
(New England Style)

8   oz. can chopped or minced clams (do not drain)
3   cups milk
2   large potatoes (diced)
3   tablespoons of margarine
1   medium onion (diced)
¼   teaspoon pepper
½   cup clam juice

Sauté onions over medium heat with just a little margarine. Add clams and clam juice and sauté for one minute.

In saucepan, boil potatoes, then drain.

Combine all ingredients together and simmer until piping hot.

Sprinkle paprika on top and serve chowder with oyster crackers.

Serves 2

CLAM CHOWDER
(Manhattan Style)

8 oz. can chopped clams (do not drain)
3 cups water
3 tablespoons of margarine
1 medium onion (diced)
¼ teaspoon pepper
½ cup clam juice
1 large can whole tomatoes
3 stalks celery, chopped
1 large carrot, chopped

Sauté onions, carrot, and celery in a little margarine over medium heat.
Add clams and clam juice and sauté for one minute.
Combine all ingredients in saucepan and simmer until piping hot.

Serve with oyster crackers.

Serves 2

FISHBURGER SOUP

1   lb. chunky whitefish (such as halibut or cod)
4   large potatoes (peeled and diced)
2   large carrots (diced)
2   stalks celery (diced)
2   tablespoons of margarine
½   cup sliced mushrooms
1   medium onion (diced)
4   cups milk
¾   cup shredded cheddar cheese
1   teaspoon pepper
1   teaspoon Italian seasoning
    Salt to taste
    Garlic powder to taste

In skillet, sauté onions and mushrooms in a little margarine. Boil potatoes and carrots (drain).
Combine all ingredients in large pot and cook over medium heat until fish is flaky.
Serve with crusty french bread or crumble croutons into soup.

Serves 6

JAMBALAYA

¼ cup chopped onion
3   tablespoons margarine
1   cup cooked shrimp
2   cups cooked rice
1   cup hot water
1   small can tomato paste
3   tablespoons chopped parsley
1   minced garlic clove
1   stalk celery (chopped)

Sauté onion, celery and garlic in a little margarine until tender.
Add remaining ingredients (except rice) and simmer until piping hot.

Serve over cooked rice.

Serves 2

SCALLOP RECIPES

Scallops are a shell fish. They are found off the coast of New England and Eastern Canada. The shell grows as large as eight inches across and the scallop is the hinge muscle inside. The muscle ranges in color from creamy white (sea scallops) to tan, pinkish or orange (bay scallops).

Scallops are an excellent source of protein and are low in fat and even though they're a shellfish, very low in cholesterol. (Check the Nutritional Chart on pages 189 and 190.)

BAY SCALLOPS are small.
SEA SCALLOPS are large.

Scallops will not flake when cooked — they will be smooth to the cut and turn creamy white.

Scallops are mild, tender sweet white meat.

To open scallops bought in the shell, after scrubbing them put in an oven at 300° until they open and you can remove the muscle.

POACHED SCALLOPS

1   lb. scallops (sea or bay)
3   tablespoons dry white wine
½   teaspoon garlic
     Season with a sprinkle of:
     Parsley, pepper, salt and paprika

Poach scallops in wine, seasoning with above spices until they are tender and turn a creamy white.

NOTE: The cooking time depends on the size of the scallop. So, just look for the translucent look to be gone. This takes only a few minutes.

Serves 2

SCALLOPED SCALLOPS

1   lb. fresh sea scallops
1   cup seasoned breadcrumbs
2   egg whites, slightly beaten
1   teaspoon black pepper
1   teaspoon parsley flakes
1   teaspoon garlic powder
1   teaspoon paprika

Preheat oven to 350°.

Lightly toss scallops in breadcrumbs, after dipping them in egg whites. Season with pepper, parsley and garlic. Sprinkle paprika on top. Spread in oiled baking dish and bake for 20 minutes or until scallops turn a bright white. Serve with lemon wedges.

Good with pineapple chunks, crisp green spinach salad and mixed vegetables.

Serves 2

Scallop Kabobs

Use wooden skewers.

Build kabob with scallops, green peppers, mushrooms, pineapple chunks and cherry tomatoes.

Grill approximately three minutes per side, basting frequently with pineapple juice and margarine. (Don't forget to spray the grill with non-stick coating so kabobs won't stick.)

Bacon-Wrapped Scallops

1   pound large scallops
1   pound bacon — cutting strips in half
Wrap raw bacon around scallop and secure it with a toothpick. Broil or bake at 350° until bacon is cooked. This recipe works great in a toaster oven too.

OYSTER RECIPES

SCALLOPED OYSTERS

1   lb. select oysters (with juice)
1   raw egg (slightly beaten)
4   cups crushed crackers
    Salt and pepper to taste

Preheat oven to 350°.

Mix above ingredients together reserving some crushed crackers. Spread in buttered casserole.
Sprinkle some of the crushed crackers on top.
Bake 30 minutes.

FRIED OYSTERS

1 lb. select oysters
1 egg (slightly beaten)
½ cup milk
2 cups crushed crackers
   salt and pepper to taste
4 cups hot cooking oil

Rinse and drain oysters.
Dip into egg & milk combination.
Season with salt and pepper.
Roll in crushed crackers.
Fry oysters until they are golden brown.
Drain on paper towels.

OYSTER STEW

1 lb. stewing oysters (undrained)
3 cups milk
¼ stick margarine
½ teaspoon celery salt
1 tablespoon worcestershire sauce

Simmer oysters with juice in skillet until oyster edges curl. Pour into saucepan with remaining ingredients and simmer until piping hot.

NOTE: Milk should be hot when adding oysters, to avoid curdling.

Serve with oyster crackers.

Serves 4

OYSTER DRESSING

1 lb. stewing oysters
1 loaf bread (coarse and shredded)
1 raw egg (slightly beaten)
1 medium chopped onion
1 stalk chopped celery
  Season with the following:
1 tablespoon sage, 1 teaspoon garlic, 1 teaspoon pepper, 1 teaspoon salt

NOTE: You may add cooked and cut-up turkey gizzards and liver if you desire.

Mix above ingredients together in large bowl. If mixture is too runny, keep adding shredded bread until it's firm enough to stuff into the turkey cavity.

AN OCEAN OF FISH

FOIL WRAPPED HALIBUT STEAKS

2   8 oz. halibut steaks
1   tablespoon margarine
¼   lemon
½   teaspoon parsley flakes
½   teaspoon paprika
¼   teaspoon garlic powder
¼   teaspoon lemon pepper
4   sliced fresh jumbo mushrooms
1   tablespoon diced green peppers
1   tablespoon shredded carrots
1   tablespoon green onion chopped

Preheat oven to 400°.

Cut foil large enough to hold each halibut steak individually (2 pc. foil for each steak). This can be cut in the shape of a fish, if you like.

Spray each piece of foil with a non-stick coating or just oil each piece of foil lightly. Dot with margarine and squeeze fresh lemon on fish. Sprinkle with above seasonings. Arrange vegetables on steak. Seal package tightly with second piece of foil. Bake 30 minutes or grill 10 minutes per side.

Serves 2

STEAMED HALIBUT

1   lb. halibut steaks
2   large carrots
6   asparagus spears
¼ lb. cauliflower
    lemon and lime juice
1   cup water

Boil water in pot or steamer.
Add fish and veggies in basket or colander. Cover pot and steam until fish flakes and veggies are tender crisp.
Serve with lemon and lime wedges.
Serve with rice and sliced tomatoes.

Serves 2

SWISS HALIBUT

This recipe is similar to the way you cook swiss steak.

In a skillet combine the following:

1   lb. halibut steaks
1   large can of whole or stewed tomatoes
1   stalk of chopped celery
1   chopped small onion
1   chopped large carrot
1   chopped green pepper
1   jar sliced mushrooms
1   tsp each of the following spices:
               garlic
               pepper
               parsley
               basil

Simmer all ingredients and add raw fish. Cover and cook until fish flakes easily with a fork.
Serves 2

HALIBUT ITALIAN STYLE

1 lb. halibut steaks
3 large cooked and skinned tomatoes
1 teaspoon Italian seasoning
½ teaspoon garlic powder
¼ cup chopped onion
¼ cup chopped green pepper
¼ cup parmesan cheese

In a skillet on low heat combine tomatoes, seasonings, onion and green pepper until mixed well. Place halibut steaks in mixture and simmer until fish is flaky. Serve with parmesan cheese sprinkled on top of fish.

Serve with pasta salad and Italian green beans

Serves 2

CAJUN STYLE CATFISH FILLETS

1 pound catfish fillets
1 cup Seafood Cajun BBQ Sauce

Line electric skillet with foil. If you're using a non-electric skillet, spray with non-stick cooking spray. Keep temperature low and be cautious of spattering. Pour in BBQ sauce. Simmer catfish fillets, covered, for 15 minutes per side. Simmer until fish is nice and flaky. If sticking occurs add a little water.

CATFISH TERIYAKI

2   8 oz. catfish fillets
1   tablespoon cooking oil
½   cup chopped green pepper
½   cup chopped onion
1   tablespoon teriyaki sauce

Heat oil in skillet. Sauté peppers and onions until half done. Add teriyaki sauce. Sauté catfish fillets in above ingredients, cooking over medium heat for approximately 15 minutes per side. Check fish for flakiness for doneness. Serve with peppers and onions poured over fish and a squeeze of fresh lemon.

Serves 2

OVEN-FRIED CATFISH FILLETS

1   lb. catfish fillets
1   cup seasoned breadcrumbs

Preheat oven to 400°.
Wet fillets and roll in breadcrumbs.
Arrange fillets in a single layer on an oiled baking pan.
Bake for 20 minutes without turning or until fish is flaky.

Serve with frozen cooked peas and mushrooms and baked potato strip (steak cut).

Serves 2

BBQ'D CATFISH FILLETS

1   lb. catfish fillets
1   cup BBQ sauce
1   cup water

Pour BBQ sauce and water into skillet.
Place fish into mixture and simmer until sauce thickens and fish is tender and flaky.

Serve with corn on the cob and sweet potatoes.

Serves 2

PEPPER FISH

1   lb. catfish fillets
1   green pepper, sliced into strips
1   teaspoon black pepper
1   tablespoon corn oil or canola
1   teaspoon paprika
½ cup sliced mushrooms
1   tablespoon soy sauce
½ cup chopped white onions

Heat canola or corn oil on low in non-stick skillet. Add veggies. Sauté peppers, onions and mushrooms until half cooked. Add catfish fillets and seasonings. Cover with lid and simmer approximately 10 minutes per side. Stir in soy sauce and simmer another 5 minutes. Fish should be flaky when done. Serve with veggies poured over top of fish.

Serve with brown rice and cauliflower.

Serves 2

BAKED COD

2   8 oz. cod fillets
1   tablespoon margarine
1   tablespoon green onion (chopped)
    wedge fresh lemon
¼   cup seasoned breadcrumbs
¼   teaspoon paprika
    dash pepper and garlic powder
¼   cup bacon bits or cooked crisp bacon
¼   cup shredded cheddar cheese

Preheat oven to 350°.
Spray baking dish with non-stick coating. Arrange fillets in dish. Dot with margarine. Squeeze on fresh lemon. Sprinkle on green onion, breadcrumbs and bacon bits. Bake 20-30 minutes. Sprinkle on cheddar cheese during the last 3 minutes of cooking. Do not turn fish over. Fish will be flaky when done.

Serves 2

BAKED COD PECAN

1   lb. cod fillets
¼   cup chopped pecans
2   egg whites
1   teaspoon lemon pepper

Preheat oven to 350°. Spray non-stick coating on baking dish. Rinse fillets. Mix pecans and egg whites together. Dip fish into mixture and arrange in baking pan. Sprinkle with lemon pepper. Bake uncovered without turning for 20-30 minutes or until fish flakes easily with a fork.

Serve with oven-fried potatoes and green beans with onions

Serves 2

MUSHROOMED FLOUNDER

1   lb. flounder fillets (without skin)
8   oz. sliced fresh mushrooms
1   cup chicken broth
2   tablespoons light margarine
½   cup wheat germ
1   fresh lemon, squeezed

Simmer flounder fillets in chicken broth until flaky.
In another skillet melt margarine.
Add mushrooms, wheat germ and lemon.
Sauté until mushrooms are tender and pour mixture over fish.

Serve with sliced cooked carrots and baked potatoes with chives.

Serves 2

HADDOCK WITH FRENCH DRESSING

1   pound haddock fillets (skinless)
½   cup French dressing
1   cup crushed buttery crackers

Preheat oven to 400°.
Dip haddock fillets in French dressing and then drain. Roll in crushed buttery crackers. Arrange fillets in baking dish that you have sprayed with non-stick coating. Bake for 20-30 minutes or until fish will flake easily with a fork.

Serves 2

PINEAPPLE MAHI-MAHI

1   lb. mahi-mahi steaks
1   cup crushed pineapple
¼   cup raisins
¼   cup shredded raw carrots

Preheat oven to 350°.
Arrange mahi-mahi in baking dish. Spread top with crushed pineapple. Scatter carrots and raisins.
Bake for 20-30 minutes or until mahi-mahi is flaky and tender.

Serve with sliced bananas and strawberries, fresh asparagus and baked potatoes topped with parmesan cheese and chives.

Serves 2

MICROWAVED ORANGE ROUGHY PARMESAN

2   8 oz. orange roughy fillets
2   tablespoons mayonnaise or salad dressing
1   tablespoon green onion (chopped)
1   tablespoon parmesan cheese
¼   cup seasoned breadcrumbs

Arrange fillets on oiled microwave-safe dish. Combine mayonnaise, green onion and parmesan cheese. Spread on each fillet. Sprinkle on paprika and breadcrumbs. Cover with waxed paper or saran wrap. Microwave on high, 2 minutes for each fillet. Do not turn fish.

Serves 2

LIMED ORANGE ROUGHY

1   lb. orange roughy fillets
2   fresh limes
1   tablespoon basil

Make a mixture of fresh squeezed lime juice and basil.
Brush onto orange roughy fillets.
Place fillets in a microwave-safe glass dish.
Cover with waxed paper.
Microwave on high for 4 minutes.
Don't forget to check fish for flakiness.

Serve with tossed green spinach salad and baked potato.

Serves 2

STEAMED PERCH

1   lb. perch fillet
1   cup water
1   fresh lemon
2   large carrots
6   asparagus spears

Boil water in pot or steamer. Place perch and veggies in basket or colander that you have placed over boiling water. Squeeze fresh lemon over all. Cover and steam until fish is flaky and veggies are tender

Serve with corn niblets and a leafy salad with vinaigrette dressing

Serves 2

POLLOCK ITALIANO

2   8 oz. pollock fillets
8   oz. can stewed tomatoes
¼   cup sliced mushrooms
¼   cup green pepper (chopped)
¼   cup parmesan cheese

Preheat oven to 350°.
Spray baking dish with non-stick coating. Arrange fillets in dish. Top with above ingredients and bake for 20-30 minutes. Check fish for flakiness for doneness.

Serves 2

PEPPERED POMFRET

1 lb. pomfret fillets (cut into strips)
1 large green pepper (cut into strips)
1 white onion (cut into chunks)
1 teaspoon chicken seasoning
1 chicken bouillon cube or teaspoon instant chicken bouillon
1 tablespoon olive oil

Sauté green pepper and onion in olive oil until they are tender crisp.

Add pomfret strips and sauté until light in color, sprinkling with chicken seasoning.

Add chicken bouillon cube and enough water to prevent fish from sticking.

Sauté for approximately 10 more minutes until veggies are tender and fish is flaky.

Serve with rice and steamed carrots.

Serves 2

OVEN-FRIED RED SNAPPER

1   lb. red snapper fillets, skinless
1   cup seasoned breading or corn meal
1   tablespoon paprika
    wedge fresh lemon

Preheat oven to 400°.
Wet fillets and roll in breading. Arrange fillets in baking dish that you have sprayed with non-stick coating or line dish with foil and then spray — (this saves clean-up time). Sprinkle fish with paprika. Squeeze on fresh lemon. Bake for 30 minutes or until fish flakes easily with a fork.

Serves 2

BLACKENED RED SNAPPER

1   lb. red snapper fillets
2   tablespoons light margarine
½   teaspoon garlic powder
½   cup cajun spice

Use your outdoor grill and make sure your coals are very hot. Spray iron skillet with non-stick coating. Mix margarine, garlic powder and cajun spice together. Brush thickly onto snapper fillets. Sear fillets in iron skillet until blackened on both sides. Reduce heat and grill until fish flakes easily when tested with a fork.

Serve with Brussels sprouts and a potato kabob

Serves 2

POTATO KABOB

2   large baking potatoes (cut into large cubes) unpeeled.
Brush potatoes with garlic and corn oil.
Skewer onto wooden skewers.
Grill 10 minutes per side or until potatoes are tender.
(You can even brush them with a cajun mixture.)

GRILLED SHARK STEAKS

2 8 oz. shark steaks
¼ cup melted margarine
¼ teaspoon garlic powder
½ teaspoon soy sauce

Spray grill with a non-stick coating. Arrange shark steaks on grill. Baste frequently with above mixture to prevent dryness. Shark will not flake when done. Test shark as you would test a pork chop by cutting into the center. When shiny raw look is gone, it's done.

Serves 2

ROLLED SOLE WITH BROCCOLI

1   pound sole fillets (firm, large fillets that you can easily roll)
1   package cooked frozen broccoli
½   cup sliced fresh mushrooms
1   tablespoon margarine
    wedge fresh lemon
½   cup shredded swiss cheese
1   tablespoon paprika

Preheat oven to 350°.
Brush sole fillets with melted margarine. Place cooked broccoli and mushrooms in center of fillet. Roll fish with filling inside and place in baking dish that you have already sprayed with oil. Secure each fish roll-up with long tooth-pick or wooden skewer. Bake 20-30 minutes and the last five minutes top with shredded swiss cheese and paprika.

FISH WINE DIVINE

1   lb. fillet of sole
1   cup white wine
½   teaspoon basil
½   cup toasted bread crumbs

In a skillet, over low heat, poach sole fillets in wine seasoning them with basil. Poach until sole flakes easily with a fork. Serve with toasted bread crumbs sprinkled over top.

Serve with broccoli and browned potatoes.

Serves 2

WHEAT GERM SOLE

1   lb. sole fillet
½ cup wheat germ
¼ teaspoon paprika
¼ teaspoon parsley flakes
1   tablespoon corn oil

Preheat oven to 350°. Spray non-stick coating on baking dish. Rinse fillets and brush lightly with canola or corn oil. Combine wheat germ and parsley. Roll fillets in dry mixture.

Arrange singly in baking dish and sprinkle with paprika. Bake for 20 minutes without turning until fish flakes easily with a fork.

Serve with steamed carrots, baked potato and cooked cabbage with low-calorie vinaigrette dressing.

Serves 2

BROILED SWORDFISH STEAKS

2 8 oz. swordfish steaks
$\frac{1}{8}$ cup olive oil
1 tablespoon Italian seasoning

Spray broiler pan or line with foil for an easy clean-up. Place steaks on pan. Brush with olive oil. Sprinkle with Italian seasoning. Broil 5-6 minutes per side. When done, fish will flake easily with a fork.

Serves 2

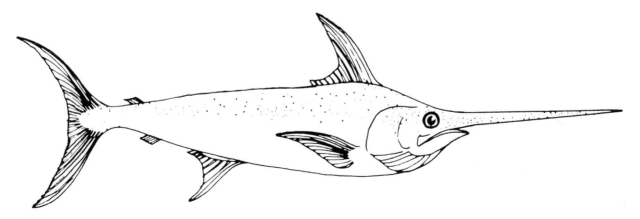

SIMMERED SWORDFISH VINAIGRETTE

1 lb. swordfish steaks
½ cup vinaigrette dressing
½ teaspoon pepper
½ teaspoon garlic powder

Mix dressing, pepper and garlic in a non-stick skillet. Add swordfish steaks and simmer approximately 15 minutes per side or until fish turns light in color and flakes easily with a fork.

Serve with boiled potatoes and broccoli.

Serves 2

GRILLED TUNA STEAKS

2   8 oz. tuna steaks
2   tablespoons melted margarine
    wedge fresh lemon
½   teaspoon garlic powder
½   teaspoon parsley flakes

Spray grill rack with a non-stick coating. Place steaks on grill. Baste frequently with above mixture. Grill tuna steaks approximately five minutes per side. Check for flakiness to tell when fish is done. (Tuna will turn light in color.)

Serves 2

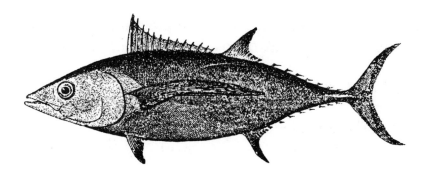

167

FRESH TUNA SALAD

1   lb. tuna steaks
½ cup chopped celery
6   chopped egg whites
1   tablespoon lemon juice
½ cup chopped onion
½ cup chopped cucumber
¼ teaspoon pepper
1   cup reduced calorie salad dressing
(optional) halved green grapes or sweet pickles, chopped

Poach tuna in skillet, covering steaks with water. Simmer tuna until it turns light in color and is very flaky. Drain and let tuna cool. Flake into a bowl and add rest of ingredients. Mix and chill.

Serve on wheat or rye bread with lettuce or just scoop tuna onto a leaf of lettuce.

Note: You can also use canned white tuna, water packed.

Serves 2

TURBOT WITH WILD RICE

1   lb. turbot fillets
1   cup white cooking wine
1   teaspoon black pepper
2   cups wild rice

Poach turbot in a skillet and add cooking wine and pepper.
Cook until turbot is tender and flaky.

Serve with wild rice and green beans with onions.

Serves 2

WILD RICE

½ cup wild rice
1 qt. boiling water
   Salt and pepper
½ lb. fresh mushrooms, sauteéd
½ teaspoon sage
   Dash thyme
1 egg yolk, beaten
1 tablespoon melted margarine

Cook rice in boiling water until tender, approximately 25 minutes. Drain and rinse. Add remaining ingredients and blend well.

Serves 2

TROUT ALMONDINE

2   whole rainbow trout (12 oz. each)
⅛ cup sliced canned mushrooms (drained)
½ cup wheat germ
¼ cup chopped almonds
1   tablespoon melted margarine
1   tablespoon lemon juice

Preheat oven to 350°.
In a bowl, mix mushrooms, wheat germ, almonds, margarine and lemon juice.
Prepare trout for stuffing (see pages 16-17).
Stuff into cavity of trout.
Bake in covered baking dish, for 30 minutes. You do not have to turn fish over.

Serve with mixed vegetables and rice

Serves 2

SEAFOOD LASAGNA

9 lasagna noodles (cooked and drained)
½ lb. crab or crab blend
½ lb. cooked salad shrimp
8 oz. low-calorie cottage cheese
1 egg white (lightly beaten)
½ teaspoon black pepper
1 cup parmesan cheese
2 8 oz. cans crushed tomatoes (drained)
1 8 oz. can cream of mushroom soup (undiluted)
8 oz. fresh sliced mushrooms
½ teaspoon garlic powder
1 tablespoon paprika
1 sliced fresh green pepper

Preheat oven to 300°.
Drop lasagna noodles into 3 qts. boiling water and cook about six minutes or until noodles are tender.

Drain and rinse with cold water.

This is a layering process.
In a 9 x 13 baking dish, spray bottom with a non-stick coating.
Arrange 3 cooked lasagna noodle strips on bottom of pan.
Spread mushroom soup over noodles.

Add $\frac{1}{2}$ crab and shrimp.
Top with green pepper and mushrooms.
Arrange 3 cooked noodles on top.
Spread on cottage cheese that you have mixed with egg white and pepper.
Add second batch of crab and shrimp.
Pour on 1 can crushed tomatoes.
Season with garlic powder.

Top with $\frac{1}{2}$ cup parmesan cheese.
Arrange 3 cooked noodles on top.
Pour on can of crushed tomatoes.
Top with remaining parmesan cheese and paprika.
Bake, covered, for 30 minutes.
Uncover lasagna and bake for another 5 minutes.
Cool before cutting into squares.

Serve with crisp green salad and toasted garlic wheat bread.

Serves 6

OREO DORY FISHWICH

2   (8 oz.) fillets oreo dory
½ cup corn meal
1   egg (lightly beaten)
1   tablespoon milk
    salt and pepper to taste

Beat egg and milk together in bowl. Season corn meal with salt and pepper in another bowl. Dip oreo dory in egg and milk mixture and then in corn meal so you have an even coating on fish. Fry fish in hot corn oil. If using a deep fat fryer use enough oil to cover fish; if using a skillet use 4 tablespoons of oil and take care to avoid spattering. Fry until fillets are golden brown on both sides and will flake when tested with a fork.

This fish is great served on a bun with lettuce, tomato, onion and tartar sauce.

Serves 2

SAUTÉED TILAPIA WITH SWEET BASIL

1   lb. tilapia fillets
1   tablespoon olive oil
¼   cup flour
¼   cup parmesan cheese
1   teaspoon dried basil or 1 tablespoon chopped fresh basil
⅛   teaspoon salt and pepper
1   tablespoon margarine
1   lemon
    paprika

Brush tilapia fillets with olive oil and set aside. Mix flour, cheese, basil, salt and pepper together in a bowl. Coat fish with this mixture. Melt margarine in skillet on very low heat. Cover and sauté fish about 10 minutes per side, squeezing on fresh lemon and sprinkling with paprika.

Serves 2

STUFFED TILAPIA

4 3 oz. tilapia fillets
1 cup seasoned breadcrumbs
¼ cup sliced mushrooms
1 tablespoon lemon juice
1 teaspoon parsley flakes or 1 tablespoon fresh chopped parsley
1 teaspoon minced garlic
   Salt and pepper to taste
1 tablespoon melted margarine

Preheat oven to 350°.
In a skillet, on low heat, sauté bread crumbs, mushrooms, lemon juice, parsley, garlic, salt and pepper together. Spray baking dish with non-stick cooking spray and arrange two fillets inside. Spoon stuffing on top of each fillet, spreading almost to the edges. Cover fish and stuffing with remaining two fillets. Brush a little margarine on the top of each piece of fish. Bake 20 minutes or until fish flakes easily with a fork.

Serves 2

GROUPER WITH SWEET PEPPERS

1   lb. grouper fillets
1   sweet bell pepper (sliced)
    Juice from 1 fresh lemon
    pepper to taste
1   teaspoon ground ginger
1   tablespoon olive oil

Sauté peppers in olive oil on low heat, adding ginger. When cooked half-way, add grouper fillets seasoning with pepper and lemon juice. Sauté fish with pepper slices until fish is flaky and peppers tender. Serve fish with peppers on top.

Serves 2

BAKED GRENADIER
(with bacon bits and red onions)

1   lb. grenadier fillets
    juice from 1 fresh lemon
    pepper to taste
1   cup bacon bits
1   sliced red onion

Preheat oven to 350°.
Arrange grenadier fillets in baking dish that you have sprayed with non-stick coating. Pepper to taste. Sprinkle on bacon bits and add slices of red onion, squeezing fresh lemon over all. Cover baking dish with foil.Bake for 20-30 minutes or until fish flakes easily with a fork.

Serves 2

LAKE SUPERIOR WHITEFISH BOIL

This recipe is very popular in Door County, Wisconsin. If cooking it for a large crowd, use a very large pot and allow ½ lb. fish per person.

Whole Lake Superior Whitefish
(cleaned, deheaded, scaled and steaked) Amount of fish used depends on number of people.

Peeled potatoes (quartered) allowing one potato per person
Peeled carrots (halved) allowing one or two carrots per person
Peeled onions (quartered) allowing ½ onion per person
Sweet corn on the cob (halved) allowing 1 or 2 per person

Fill large pot half to three-quarters full with water seasoned with lemon-pepper and garlic clove. Add one fish bouillon cube per quart of water making a good fish stock.

Add vegetables and cook until half tender. Add whitefish steaks and cook slowly until fish and veggies are tender.

Serve piping hot with hard rolls or corn bread.

SALMON RECIPES

SALMON

Did you ever think about baking a whole salmon for a party? Well, let's do one!

Start with a 4 pound head-on fresh salmon.

You may want to have the clerk butterfly and bone fish.

Oil the outside of the fish so it won't stick to the pan. Brush inside of fish with a mixture of margarine, minced garlic, parsley and lemon juice.

Fold over and bake in a 350° oven.

Bake 10 minutes for every inch of thickness, measuring at the thickest part of the fish.

Approximate baking time is 1 to 2 hours. But to tell when your fish is done, the skin should peel back easily and, unless you had it boned, when tested with a fork the backbone inside should lift very easily.

Remove head and tail before serving.

Serve salmon cold, as an appetizer, with a dill sauce.

NOTE: A whole salmon makes a beautiful centerpiece. Garnish your tray with parsley, lemon and cherry tomatoes.

Save That Backbone

When you lift the backbone out of the whole salmon, notice all the salmon left on it. Don't throw it away because we're going to use it in our next recipe!

Salmon Dip

Remove all salmon from backbone, Add softened cream cheese and chopped green onion and 2 or 3 tablespoons drippings from pan salmon was cooked in. This is a wonderful spread to dip breadsticks into or to stuff into celery sticks.

Dill Sauce

Make a white sauce in a saucepan by combining: 1 cup milk; 2 tablespoons flour; 1 teaspoon butter or margarine; $\frac{1}{2}$ teaspoon lemon juice; 1 teaspoon dill; pepper to taste. Stir over medium heat until thickened. Serve warm or cold with salmon.

SALMON SALAD

1   lb. cooked and flaked salmon
8   oz. cooked rotini noodles (drained)
1   cup Italian dressing
1   teaspoon pepper
1   teaspoon seasoned salt
2   large chopped fresh tomatoes
1   large green pepper, chopped
½   cup chopped green onion

Combine above ingredients and chill one hour before serving.

It's great on wheat crackers or as a side salad on a crisp leaf of lettuce.

EASY SALMON SALAD

My Mom made the best salmon salad in three easy steps:

1. Cooked fresh or canned salmon (drained)
2. Salad dressing or mayo
3. Frozen uncooked peas (thawed)

Mix and add a little pepper.

LITTLE SALMON PATTIES

1   cup shredded salmon (cooked) fresh or canned.
1   raw egg (lightly beaten)
1   medium chopped onion
1   teaspoon pepper
1   teaspoon garlic powder
1   cup cracker meal
½   cup parmesan cheese

Combine all ingredients in bowl and mix.
Shape into little patties.
Bake at 325° until browned or sauté in a little margarine in the skillet on low heat until browned.
Sprinkle with parmesan cheese.

Makes 4 patties

A SAUCE FOR BAKED SALMON

1 cup fat free mayo
   dash salt
1 teaspoon Grey Poupon mustard
   dash curry powder
1 tablespoon lemon juice
1 teaspoon horseradish
   dash fresh ginger
1 tomato
⅛ cup sauterne

Preheat oven to 350°.
Combine all of the above ingredients in a blender and puree.
Pour this on salmon fillets or salmon steaks adding freshly ground pepper. Bake until salmon flakes easily with a fork. Approximately 20-30 minutes.

Thank my dear friend Carol Kolhouser for this recipe.

A SALMON SAUCE FOR SPAGHETTI

1   lb. skinned salmon fillet
8   oz. pkg. spaghetti
1   14 oz. can crushed tomatoes
8   oz. sliced mushrooms
¼   cup chopped green onions
¼   cup chopped green peppers
1   teaspoon garlic powder
1   teaspoon sweet basil
¼   teaspoon black pepper

Poach salmon covered with water until salmon is opaque and flakes easily with a fork.
Let cool.
Simmer tomatoes with veggies and seasoning until mixed well.
Add flaked salmon and heat 15 minutes.
Cook spaghetti in boiling water until tender.
Drain.
Put spaghetti onto plate and pour sauce on top.

Serve with spinach salad and wheat breadsticks

EASY SALMON

1 lb. salmon steaks
½ cup olive oil vinaigrette
½ teaspoon lemon pepper

Preheat oven to 350°. Mix vinaigrette and lemon pepper. Arrange steaks in non-stick baking dish. Spread mixture on top and bake for 20-30 minutes without turning. Check fish for flakiness.

Serve with fresh fruit cup, baked potato and spinach.

SALMON OR TUNA PASTA SALAD

1   cup cooked salmon (fresh or canned) flaked
or 1 cup canned tuna
1   cup cooked and cooled rotini pasta
½ teaspoon garlic powder
¼ cup pimento
¼ cup chopped green pepper
⅛ cup chopped green onion
⅛ teaspoon basil
½ cup wheat germ
½ cup low-calorie Italian dressing or olive oil vinaigrette

Combine above ingredients and add to cooked pasta. Chill 3 to 4 hours to lock flavor in.

This is best when made a day ahead.

If you're watching your calories, cholesterol and fat intake — this chart is for you.

Per 3 oz. cooked serving:

Fish	Calories	Cholesterol	Fat
Carp	138	71 mg.	6.1 g.
Catfish	99	49 mg.	3.6 g.
Clams	126	57 mg.	1.7 g.
Cod	89	47 mg.	0.7 g.
Flounder	99	58 mg.	1.3 g.
Grouper	100	40 mg.	1.1 g.
Haddock	95	63 mg.	0.8 g.
Halibut	119	35 mg.	2.5 g.
Lobster	83	61 mg.	0.5 g.
Mahi-mahi	72	62 mg.	0.6 g.
Monkfish	65	21 mg.	1.3 g.
Orange Roughy	59	17 mg.	0.6 g.
Oysters	58	46 mg.	2.1 g.
Perch	103	46 mg.	1.8 g.
Pollock	96	82 mg.	1.0 g.

Red Snapper	109	40 mg.	1.5 g.
Salmon (Sockeye)	130	37 mg.	6.2 g.
Scallops	75	28 mg.	0.7 g.
Shark	111	43 mg.	3.8 g.
Shrimp	113	163 mg.	1.8 g.
Sole	99	58 mg.	1.3 g.
Surimi (Crab/Lobster Blend)	84	26 mg.	0.7 g.
Swordfish	132	43 mg.	4.4 g.
Rainbow Trout	128	62 mg.	3.7 g.
Tuna	156	42 mg.	5.3 g.
Turbot	81	41 mg.	2.5 g
Lake Superior Whitefish	176	70 mg.	5.0 g

Tilapia — n/a
Oreo Dory — n/a
Grenadier — n/a

Seafood is a good source of protein and it is lower in fat and cholesterol than other meats.

I recommend putting seafood in your diet at least twice a week because it is a good source of vitamins, phosphorus, potassium and iron.

SOME OFTEN-ASKED QUESTIONS

DEAR FISHLADY,

Whenever I buy shrimp, I also buy cocktail sauce to go with it.

My problem is, there's always sauce left over — so I put it in the fridge until the next time. But when I need to use it, I feel it's too old. Should I just throw the leftover sauce away?

Signed,

WASTEFUL

DEAR WASTEFUL,

You don't have to be! Many years ago, someone told me what to do with that leftover cocktail sauce, and it's really a great idea.

The next time you make a batch of meat loaf, instead of using ketchup — use that leftover cocktail sauce. It really adds zip!

DEAR FISHLADY,

If I overcook my shrimp or lobster, do I have to throw it away? It just seems too tough to eat!

Signed,

OVERDOING IT

DEAR OVERDOING IT,

Well, your meal may be ruined, but you don't have to throw it away. Just freeze it for another day. When you thaw it out, grind or chop finely for your next dip, salad, stew or quiche.

DEAR FISHLADY,

Should I use shellfish, such as clams, mussels or oysters if the shell is open? Also, how do I store them to keep them fresh?

Signed,

WINKING AT ME

DEAR WINKING,

If the shells are open, they're probably dried out, so I wouldn't recommend using them. Shells should be closed tightly when you catch or purchase them.

To keep shell fish "fresh," never rinse them in water — this will kill them. Instead, wash them off with a cool, damp cloth and store them in the coldest part of the refrigerator in a paper bag until ready to use. They don't keep very long though, so use them in a few days.

Never freeze them in the shell!

After you take them out of the shell — freezing is OK.

DEAR FISHLADY,

I purchased a fresh whole cooked lobster and I'd like to know how to tell if it's really "fresh."

Signed,

LOBSTER LOVER

DEAR LOBSTER,

Just check the tail! If it springs back — it's fresh! Also, the meat in the tail should be bright white. The claw meat is great for eating too — but you'll need a nut cracker. The meat is very sweet. Dip it in drawn butter.

DEAR FISHLADY,

Whenever I make oyster stew, my oysters always seem like they're raw. Shouldn't they be just a little more chewy?

Signed,

IN A STEW

DEAR STEW,

You need to par cook your oysters before adding them to your stew. Here's how: Pour oysters (liquid and all) into a skillet and simmer until the edges of the oysters curl. Next — add the oysters (and liquid) to milk, butter, celery salt and worcestershire sauce and pepper and cook until piping hot.

Did you know that in prehistoric times, oysters were a foot long? Just imagine the pearl! Fred Flintstone probably had it drilled for his bowling ball!

DEAR FISHLADY,

How do I tell if I'm eating a real scallop and not just a round piece of whitefish? Also, why are some of the scallops orange in color?

Signed,

SCALLOPING GOURMET

DEAR SCALLOPING,

When cooked, scallops do not flake as do most fish. They're smooth to the cut. And don't be alarmed if you see an orange scallop. That's just the female.

DEAR FISHLADY,

Do live lobsters really scream when you drop them into boiling water? It tears me up!

Signed,

IN PIECES

DEAR IN PIECES,

Glue yourself back together! What you are hearing are the gasses escaping. If you'd feel better — after bringing your live lobster home — just put it in the freezer until ready to cook. It does seem more humane.

DEAR FISHLADY,

After I boil shrimp, my kids could use them to bounce off the walls — why so rubbery!

Signed,

BOILING MAD

DEAR BOILING,

Cool down and don't give up! All you're doing is boiling your shrimp a little too long. So cut down your cooking time.
To tell when shrimp is done, look for the color to be bright pink and the translucent look gone. Just leave them in the water until they curl half way — but not into a tight ball!

DEAR FISHLADY,

Is that "fake stuff" called "crab or lobster blend" real? Do I need to cook it before I use it in a recipe calling for crab or lobster?

Signed,

FAKED OUT AND IN DOUBT

DEAR FAKED,

No fooling, it's real! But not quite 100%. It's more like 33% real crab or lobster, combined with pollock (which is a whitefish). It sells for a fourth of what real crab or lobster sells for and you can make any dish as "crabby" as you like because it's fully cooked.
To me, it tastes better than the real thing and it's great used in dips, salads, casseroles, stir-frys and quiches. Or just plain, dipped in cocktail sauce for an appetizer.